Hope, Home, & Holidays

Winter Devotionals Inspired by God's Creation

Hope, Home, & Holidays

Winter Devotionals Inspired by God's Creation

ANDREA ROBINSON

McGahan

Hope, Home, & Holidays: Winter Devotionals Inspired by God's Creation

Rooted & Flourishing *Devotional Series*

Copyright © 2022 by Andrea L. Robinson

MCGAHAN PUBLISHING HOUSE | LYNCHBURG, TENNESSEE

www.mphbooks.com

Requests for information should be sent to:

info@mphbooks.com

_____

Cover Design by Marynn Spurlock & Andrew Waters

Photos & Graphics by Kaleigh Madison LLC

ISBN 978-1-951252-20-5

To Wesley, Asher, and Abel: for allowing

our family life to become an open book

Contents

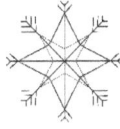

Acknowledgements

I'm overwhelmed by the love and support of the people God has placed in my life. Words can't express the extent to which I am thankful for my family and friends. To Wesley, you are my North Star, soulmate, and best friend. From emotional support to devotional feedback to household upkeep, I couldn't function without you. To Asher, my favorite surprise and faithful assistant, thank you for remaining patient and peaceful despite my frenetic pace. Your attention to detail and organizational skills equip me to accomplish exponentially more than I could alone. To Abel, the life of the party and heart of our family, your love keeps my priorities in order and gives me the confidence to reach goals beyond my imagination. To all of my family and friends, thank you for allowing me to share your best moments, worst moments, and everything in between. Your encouragement strengthens me more than you know, and my life is enriched because you are part of it. To my dear friends Tom and Lisa Buckle and Doug and Melissa Sittason, thank you for remaining faithful friends despite my periodic disappearances due to devotional writing. To Lynn Ferrell, you are a constant source of wisdom in my life, and your feedback on these devotionals will bless each person who reads them. To Hollie Sipe, I treasure your words of encouragement as much as your editing skills, which are substantial. Both have made this volume substantially better. To the many friends who've supported the launch of Rooted and Flourishing—Amanda, Amy, Brian, Bridget, Brittani, Jessy, Karen, Kim, Laura, Tonya, Mike, and Veneranda—I'm honored by your faith in these devotionals and your willingness to share them with others. To my graphic designer/photographer/media expert, Kaleigh McGinn, I'm thankful for your endless patience and awed at your ability to make my wild ideas look professional. To my pastors, Spencer and Ellen Beach, thank you for continuing to champion my work and pour wisdom into my life. Your leadership has equipped me to grow in every aspect of my life and ministry. For Caleb Poston and McGahan Publishing, I want to express sincere gratitude once again. Your dialogue and feedback have brought my vision for these devotionals to life and made them better along the way. Finally, thank you to Jesus, my Lord and Friend. I pray that my own imperfect efforts honor you and edify your people.

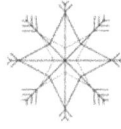

Introduction & Instructions

Hello friends,

If you read the autumn volume of Rooted & Flourishing, I hope you feel like you're returning to spend time with a friend. With each devotional I write, I imagine sharing my stories with you face-to-face, and I pray for God to work in your heart. As my winter devotionals revolve around *Hope, Home, & Holidays*, I invite you to come into my home, sit by the fire, and listen to some lessons I've learned through the years.

In case you this is the first book you're reading in the Rooted & Flourishing series, let me briefly introduce myself. I am a wife, mom, pastor, scholar, adventurer, fitness fanatic, and avid gardener. I'm far from perfect, but I love Jesus, I love to learn, and I seize every day with joy. Despite my qualifications as a scholar, I'm quite irresponsible and impulsive. Nonetheless, God allows me to serve Him in ways that astound me.

In January 2020 as I was fasting, I felt God compelling me to write a series of devotions inspired by nature. Although I was excited about the prospect of writing devotionals, I simply wasn't sure when I would have time to write them. As a pastor, wife, and mom of two boys, my schedule didn't exactly provide large blocks of writing time. Unbeknownst to me, God was already orchestrating the circumstances under which I would be writing devotionals on a daily basis.

Introductions & Instructions

As we now know, 2020 was the year in which we encountered the coronavirus, a quarantine, and an unprecedented degree of isolation. In an effort to encourage our church family, our church staff decided to produce daily devotionals, and I lead the project. Initially, I didn't make the connection between the devotionals God was calling me to write and the devotionals I was writing for our church. As time passed, however, I realized that God was helping me sow the seeds of my devotional project.

You now hold in your hands the winter installment of the Rooted & Flourishing series. Although many of the devotionals in this volume focus on family, you'll also learn much about God's creation and many lessons from it. As you read devotions that reflect the ebb and flow of the natural world, I pray that you become more deeply rooted in God's presence and flourish in your life's journey.

Before you begin, allow me to offer a few suggestions. Each day, I've provided a devotional, a brief prayer, and a prompt for reflection, meditation, or application. I pray that each will serve as a launching point for further prayer, introspection, and growth.

I've also included blank space for journaling. I will occasionally suggest journaling cues, but the space is primarily for you to write your thoughts on how the devotional impacted you or what God is impressing upon your soul. As you pray, meditate, and journal, take time to listen for the still, small voice of God. Give him permission to uproot any weeds in the garden of your life, create fertile soil for new growth, and plant the seeds of his will.

Be sure to connect with me at **www.AndreaLeighRobinson.org** and on social media. I have additional content and interactive opportunities waiting for you!

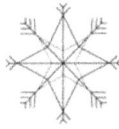

Day 1
'Tis the Season

Life flows in seasons, and winter is upon us. While I don't enjoy cold temperatures, I do love the holiday season. As soon as Halloween ends, I go into full holiday mode. I've always savored the delectable meals, meaningful gatherings, and cozy naps of Thanksgiving. I've always relished the inviting scents, twinkling lights, and festive music of Christmas. My enchantment with the holiday season far outweighs my aversion to the cold.

In fact, each season of life is characterized by its own blessings and challenges. Harsh winter weather and seasonal stresses are accompanied by celebrations, festivities and joyful gatherings. Similarly, the coming spring brings warmth, beauty, and growth along with a plethora of biting bugs and pollen. Clearly, we don't live in a perfect world, but we can make the most of each season.

The author of Ecclesiastes shares his own meditation on making the most of life.

God has made everything beautiful for its own time.
He has planted eternity in the human heart, but
even so, people cannot see the whole scope of God's
work from beginning to end. So I concluded there is
nothing better than to be happy and enjoy ourselves
as long as we can. And people should eat and drink

> *and enjoy the fruits of their labor, for these are gifts*
> *from God.*
> ### *Ecclesiastes 3:11–14*

As humans with limited knowledge and foresight, we can find joy in each day even when we don't understand God's plan. Some seasons are characterized by a greater measure of blessing and some by a greater measure of trial, but God is at work in each. The author of Ecclesiastes, therefore, encourages us to be happy, enjoy life, and revel in God's gifts. Less-than-enjoyable moments of toil and labor will always be part of life, but our load will feel lighter when we take every opportunity to celebrate God's generous provision.

Over the next few months, you and I will talk about making the most of each season. Since we are approaching the season of Christ's advent, we'll discuss how his birth, life, death, and resurrection enable us to live with peace, joy, and confidence. We'll seek to follow in his footsteps by learning about compassion and kindness. We'll also spend a good deal of time with Jesus' forefather David. We can learn much about God's faithfulness from the life of the flawed, but fully devoted king. Finally, since our life of faith can only grow to maturity in the context of relationships, we'll discuss strategies for healthy communication, forgiveness, and selfless love.

As we approach this holiday season, I pray you experience the fullness of Christ's joy and peace. More importantly, though, I pray you experience profound spiritual growth and a deeper understanding of Jesus' love than ever before.

Lord, thank you for guiding me through every season of life. Empower me to recognize the blessings in every season, even difficult ones. Help me learn to live with peace and joy that endures despite my circumstances. As I enter this new season, I ask you to search my heart and refine my soul. Give me endurance, perseverance, and fortitude as I seek to follow your will. Grow my faith as I draw nearer to my Savior. As I learn from the example of Christ, teach me to offer selfless service, unconditional love, and perpetual forgiveness. Fill my heart to overflowing with your love so that I can bless and encourage others. In Jesus' name, Amen.

Personal Reflection

Make a list of people with whom you have meaningful relationships or frequent contact in your current season of life. Whether your interactions are a source of joy or frustration, thank God for each individual and ask God to bless them. Pray for God's guidance as you seek to cultivate relationships that are healthy and holy in every sphere of your life.

_____

_____

_____

_____

_____

_____

_____

_____

Day 1

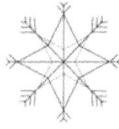

Day 2
Deck the Halls — Part 1

Yesterday, I mentioned that I love the holidays. My older son, Asher, is likewise obsessed and is an enabling accomplice. Each year on November 1, we begin a month-long process of decoration and preparation for Christmas.

Stage one consists of outdoor lights. We cover every tree, bush, and surface in white lights. For variety, we also spotlight cute wintry creatures, such as a fox, dog, deer, and snowman. Inevitably, we'll need extra lights or decor and end up making last-minute trips to the store. Even my husband Wesley, who claims to hate decorating, takes part in hanging lights on the house with the excuse that he is only helping because the gutters need cleaning. Between Wesley, Asher and I, the outdoor prep usually takes a few days to complete.

Stage two of the operation takes place indoors. We bring boxes and bins of decor down from the attic, then proceed to fill every room with holiday spirit. We arrange multiple nativity sets, substitute regular towels with Christmas towels, scatter Christmas blankets, and pillows throughout the house, and replace normal wall decor with Christmas-themed art. We replace the books on the entertainment center with an old-fashioned Christmas village. We also decorate the mantelpiece with colorful lights, fake snow, and a variety of Hallmark ceramics that light up and play music. Finally, we hang adorable stockings featuring snow-men and penguins.

Day 3

Stage three of Christmas prep consists of decorating the tree. For someone who doesn't like Christmas decorating, Wesley is oddly insistent on a live tree, so we all go out in search of the perfect one. Once we make our selection, bring the tree home, and set it up in the living room, we break open the eggnog and turn on holiday music. With the atmosphere prepared, we drench the tree in colorful lights, garland, and ornaments. Most of the ornaments are glass balls, but we also have assorted snow-men, dogs, birds, and other nature-related trinkets.

If you think our Christmas decor sounds like an insane explosion of light and color, you are correct! We are less concerned with sophisticated aesthetics than the sentiment attached to each decoration. Moreover, the time we spend together is monumentally more important than the result of our decorating spree.

Our Christmas preparation has a purpose. As we decorate, we strengthen family bonds and celebrate the blessings of God. The joy that fills our home is a reminder that life is about more than work, school, and accomplishments. We don't necessarily forget that life can be hard, but the celebration bolsters our spirits and strengthens our hearts for the next season. Furthermore, as we spend time together, our boys Asher and Abel learn the value of balancing seasons of work and seasons of celebration. They learn that hard work actually facilitates the freedom to rest, relax, and enjoy the fruit of our labors.

Above all, our preparation is an expression of the joy that arises from our relationship with Jesus. As we decorate together, we celebrate his birth, acknowledge his sacrifice, and express our gratitude. However, the reason that we can enjoy a meaningful, peaceful and joyful Christmas season together is that our celebration is a continuation of the bonds we foster throughout the year. Ever since the boys were babies, we have prayed and studied together as a family. I fully believe that our family devotions are the reason we can claim the following verses:

Lord, thank you for strengthening, supporting, and restoring me in your perfect timing. Help me to trust in your power and sovereignty. Help me to focus upon your love and grace rather than fixate on my problems. Show me what I can learn from every trial or difficulty I face, whether big or small. In Jesus' name, Amen.

Personal Reflection

If God immediately rescued us from every trial, we would miss out on valuable life lessons and growth opportunities. What can you learn from your current trials and problems? What lessons has God taught you through past trials, for which you can now give thanks? What can you do to better equip yourself to successfully navigate trials in the future?

_____

_____

_____

_____

_____

_____

_____

_____

_____

Day 3

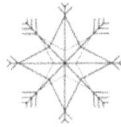

Day 3
Deck the Halls — Part 2

Yesterday, I described the holiday decorating spree that takes place in my home prior to Christmas. When the kids were young, our decor was simple. Over the years, our process has expanded and became increasingly complex. As the boys have grown, we've added more festive elements and given Asher and Abel increasing leeway to handle fragile decorations.

Now that the boys are almost grown, they can hang lights and set out decor quite efficiently. At 15 and 17, respectively, Abel and Asher are almost six feet tall. They can hang lights on tall branches and place decorations on high shelves more easily than I can.

For me, having two man-sized boys is often disorienting. It seems impossible that my baby boys are bigger than I am. I don't understand how the years have slipped by so quickly. Yet, I'm thankful that God helped me set priority on family time early in our lives.

As a task-oriented, goal-driven individual, peeling myself away from work can be excruciating. However, my family has always taken priority. When pursuing my master's degree, I took a light course load to ensure I had time with my boys. Then, I then took a five-year break between my master's and PhD work because I wanted to treasure every moment with Abel and Asher before they started school. Over the years, I've turned down speaking engagements, writing opportunities, job offerings, and social activities to invest in my children. And I don't regret giving up a single thing.

The Psalmist speaks to the importance of managing our time wisely. In Psalm 90:12, he says, "Teach us to realize the brevity of life, so that we may grow in wisdom." If you are over 40 like me, you know that the years fly past more quickly than you can imagine. If you are younger, I hope you will take my word for it. Set priorities and live by them. Set boundaries and don't break them.

I'm not saying that you will never make an exception to your rules. On one particular Christmas, we didn't put up any decor except a tree. At that time, I was in the end stages of dissertation writing and within months of completing my PhD. Because I had already invested in my family, they knew they were my ultimate priority. They also knew that I was in a once-in-a-lifetime season that required sacrifice from everyone.

On the other hand, if your schedule is always in a hair-on-fire, emergency-lights-flashing state, adjustments need to be made. Otherwise, your life will slip by and you'll miss out on the best parts. Let's lean into God's wisdom, set healthy boundaries, and live by our priorities.

Lord, thank you for providing wisdom in abundance. Grant me a greater measure of wisdom so that I can make the most of each day. Help me to set godly priorities and live by them. Show me how to set healthy boundaries and remain within them. Help me to prioritize people over tasks and relationships over accomplishments. Help me see my life through the perspective of eternity and recognize the brevity of my life on earth. Guide me as I seek to invest in pursuits that have lasting value. In Jesus' name, Amen

Personal Reflection

Write out your priorities then write out your typical daily routine. Evaluate how well your routine aligns with your priorities. Prayerfully create one or two new boundaries to help you better align your priorities and your schedule. Be sure to write down your thoughts because we'll review them next month when we revisit the discipline of setting healthy priorities.

_____

_____

_____

_____

_____

_____

_____

_____

_____

_____

_____

_____

_____

_____

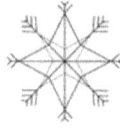

Day 4
Smiley the Elf

Each year on December 1, our family is visited by a holiday elf named Smiley. Like most Christmas elves, he entertains himself during the night and leaves amusing displays for the family to view in the morning. Sometimes he even leaves small gifts, mugs of cocoa, and encouraging notes. He also has an evil twin named Yelims, as well as two cousins, Donk and Tonk, naughty gnomes who make mischief and messes.

As much fun as we have with Smiley, Asher and Abel are long past the age where they believed he has magical powers and lives with Santa. The last few years, my boys have even helped the elves and gnomes make mischief at night, creating inventive displays for Smiley, Yelims, Donk, and Tonk. Now, our whole family enjoys the tongue-in-cheek fun we have with our holiday elves and gnomes.

At one point, however, we weren't sure if Asher was ever going to admit Smiley wasn't real. He clung to the false belief with faith and fervor, afraid that the fun would end if he acknowledged the truth. Fortunately, he now loves participating in the nightly elf/gnome mischief instead of being a passive observer.

Asher's transition to a more mature approach to Christmas brings to mind Paul's teaching about growth in Christ. In 1 Corinthians 13:11, Paul explains, "When I was a child, I spoke and thought and reasoned as a child. But when I grew up, I put away childish things." Paul highlights the need for us to grow out of immature thoughts, behaviors, and actions.

Releasing immature beliefs is difficult because they feel familiar, comfortable, and safe. Although they may serve us for a time, false truths will also stymie our growth. Instead, Christ empowers us to understand the deeper truths of Scripture and be transformed by them. Paul affirms that as we mature, our Savior "makes us more and more like him as we are changed into his glorious image," (2 Corinthians 3:18b). We gain nothing by clinging to childish reasoning, but when we release our immature beliefs, we gain the glory of Christ.

Lord, thank you for equipping me for continual growth. Expose any false beliefs to which I am clinging and give me the courage to relinquish them. Help me replace immature patterns of thought and behavior with the wisdom of Scripture. Teach me to reason with maturity and accept the truth. Transform me increasingly into your likeness and empower me to reflect your glory. In Jesus' name, Amen.

Personal Reflection

Prayerfully examine your strongly held beliefs and ask God to show you any false beliefs to which you are clinging. Reflect on the following questions and write your thoughts below.

- Can you explain why you believe what you believe?
- How is your reasoning based on Scripture?
- Which (if any) tenants of Scripture do you struggle to accept and why?
- Which (if any) secular beliefs do you accept even though they contradict Scripture? Why?

Day 4

Assessing your own beliefs can be exceptionally difficult. You may want to consult with a trusted mentor or spiritual advisor as you evaluate your core beliefs.

_____

_____

_____

_____

_____

_____

_____

_____

_____

_____

_____

_____

_____

_____

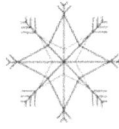

Day 5
The Most Wonderful Time of the Year

Christmas is, in my opinion, the most wonderful time of the year. Unfortunately, the holidays are also a season during which many people feel overwhelmed and depressed. There are so many decorations to hang, presents to buy, and parties to attend that we rush around without savoring the season. We may also struggle to enjoy the festivities because we miss loved ones who have passed away. Further, celebration can feel discordant in the light of all the national and global strife. When our hearts are heavy from our own losses and the suffering of others, joy feels unattainable. However, you can take heart because you were especially created "for such a time as this" (Esther 4:14).

Let me explain by telling you about reindeer. Reindeer, also known as Caribou, are remarkable animals. This species of deer lives in the Arctic tundra, one of the coldest regions in the world. Outside of mating season, reindeer are placid and peaceful. Yet their immense size gives them an advantage and helps them defend against predators. The males can grow to over 400 pounds, 7 feet long, and 5 feet tall at the shoulder. Including the head and antlers, a male caribou can grow nearly 10 feet tall!

The most interesting traits of the reindeer are their cold weather adaptations. Their noses are equipped with a multitude of small capillaries that warm frigid air before it enters the lungs. Their noses also boast a keen sense of smell, which equips them to locate food buried under ice and snow. They are also the only species of deer to grow hair on their noses.

In fact, caribou have hair all over their bodies. During the coldest winter months, reindeer grow two coats, a dense inner layer and an outer layer of hollow hairs. The hollow hairs serve as an effective layer of insulation against freezing temperatures. The hair even grows on the bottom of a reindeer's feet and makes it possible to walk on icy surfaces without slipping.

The point I'm trying to make is that reindeer are perfectly suited to their environment. In a similar manner, God has equipped you to thrive wherever you are (2 Timothy 3:17). God chose you to be conceived by your parents. He allowed you to be born in a certain time and location. He brought you into a specific culture and period in history for a specific purpose.

Likewise, God planned the details surrounding Jesus' birth to the smallest detail. Hundreds of years before Mary conceived, Micah prophesied, "But you, O Bethlehem Ephrathah, are only a small village among all the people of Judah. Yet a ruler of Israel, whose origins are in the distant past, will come from you on my behalf," (Micah 5:2).

Just as God prepared Jesus for a specific place and purpose, he has prepared you. The circumstances of your birth weren't a surprise to God, and neither are the events happening in the world today. Yet, you don't have to worry because your Father is both wise enough and powerful enough to manage the chaos.

As he cares for our world, he calls, equips, and empowers you and I to be his agents of change, healing, and peace. When we trust and obey our Father, we can take assurance that God is sovereign and that he has a good plan. When we rest in that faith, every day is an opportunity for celebration, especially in the season of Christ's birth!

Lord, thank you for creating me for a specific purpose at a specific time in history. Teach me to have greater faith in your sovereign knowledge and power. Forgive me for doubting your goodness when bad things happen in the world. I pray that you would work through me to make a difference. Give me opportunities to ease the suffering of others. Help me to live purposefully and walk in obedience. Fill my heart with joy as I follow you. I look forward to the day when you return and end suffering for eternity. In Jesus' name, Amen

Personal Reflection

Sometimes we get so caught up in the busyness of the season that we lose sight of our Savior. How can you honor his birth by serving him during the Christmas season? How can you follow his example of helping those in need? Brainstorm a few ideas and write them below. Prayerfully decide on at least one way you can serve those who need it most over the next couple of weeks.

_____

_____

_____

_____

_____

_____

Day 5

Day 6
Under the Mistletoe — Part 1

What does mistletoe have in common with the government? By the end of this devo, you'll be able to answer that question. Let's talk first about mistletoe.

Mistletoe is an attractive evergreen plant with small white berries. Because it can flourish in harsh winter conditions, the plant has traditionally been associated with health and virility. Ancient Greeks believed that mistletoe had both aphrodisiacal and medicinal properties. Although mistletoe isn't actually an aphrodisiac, it does have significant medical benefits. Mistletoe extracts can be used to boost the immune system, fight cancer, reduce stress, and improve cardiovascular function.

In first-century Europe, Druids believed the plant had magical abilities to enhance fertility in both humans and animals. The fertility rites of the Druids evolved into the practice of kissing under the mistletoe, which was thought to ensure marital union during the Middle Ages. Eventually, the superstitious beliefs surrounding mistletoe fell away and the plant has simply become part of today's lighthearted holiday tradition.

In the animal kingdom, mistletoe is more than a fun tradition. The plant is a valuable source of food for forest dwellers. Since mistletoe is one of the few plants that thrives in winter, its berries are available when other sources of nutrition are scarce. In fact, nearly every type of mammal and bird in the forest dines upon the hearty plant.

As a food supply for animals, a fun holiday tradition, and a treatment for various illnesses, mistletoe is an exceptional plant. However, mistletoe also has less than desirable qualities. While the leaves of the plant are medicinal, the berries are poisonous to humans. In small amounts, the berries probably won't kill you, but they will cause severe gastrointestinal distress.

Just as disconcerting, mistletoe is a parasite. When a mistletoe seed germinates, it sends root-like tendrils into the bark of its host, through which the plant siphons nutrients and water. If the mistletoe continues to grow, it will eventually cause the death of its host. In fact, mistletoe is so parasitic that it is termed a hyperparasite. Mistletoe will latch onto other mistletoe plants, creating a chain of parasites that rapidly drain the host.

So, what does mistletoe have in common with the government? Like mistletoe, the government is complex. Governments draw resources from their population, but they also provide important services and beneficial legislation. Sometimes governments misuse resources, but they also provide essential infrastructure and administration that keeps our communities running smoothly.

In short, most governments are a mixture of good and bad. Most rulers aren't completely evil, but neither are they completely virtuous. Most policies aren't created out of nefarious motives, but neither are they established for totally altruistic reasons. Governments are imperfect because they are comprised of imperfect people.

Governments in the Greco-Roman period of the New Testament were just as complex as they are today. Accordingly, the scriptural instructions to Christ followers regarding the government have not changed. Paul instructs, "Everyone must submit to governing authorities. For all authority comes from God, and those in positions of authority have been placed there by God. So anyone who rebels against authority is rebelling against what God has instituted, and they will be punished," (Romans 13:1). Paul offers strong words about our response to the government.

The apostle's command to submit can be hard to accept for many people in our politically divisive climate. Yet, whether or not we agree with the policies of our government or approve of those who run it, we are commanded to submit. Yet, just as the government itself is complex, our response, at times, may be likewise complex. Therefore, we'll resume the subject again tomorrow. In the meantime, let's pray.

Lord, thank you for your power and sovereignty over the whole earth. Help me to trust you even when my country and my world feel unstable. Help me trust you even when rulers make decisions with which I disagree. Give me the discernment to respond wisely when rulers make decisions that are contrary to your word. Give me the courage to respond in a manner that honors you. Give me greater compassion for my government leaders and help me see them as imperfect people who need your grace. In Jesus' name, Amen

Personal Reflection

Take some time to pray for your local government today. Pray for your mayor, city council, school superintendent, police chief, and fire chief. If you don't know the names of your leaders, look them up so that you can pray for them specifically. Pray that your government officials will accept Christ and grow in their faith. Pray that they will lead wisely with the best interests of the people at heart. Pray that God will guard them from the deception of the enemy and protect them from harm. Pray that God would use them to implement policies that honor him and benefit your community.

Day 6

_____

_____

_____

_____

_____

_____

_____

_____

_____

_____

_____

_____

_____

_____

_____

_____

_____

_____

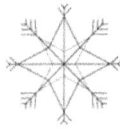

Day 7
Under the Mistletoe — Part 2

Yesterday we talked about mistletoe, which is a multifaceted plant with both desirable and damaging properties. While the leaves have substantial medicinal value, the berries are poisonous to humans. While mistletoe is a dietary staple for forest animals, it is also a parasitic plant that can kill large swaths of trees.

Like mistletoe, the government is also a complex entity. Governments fulfill an essential role in the well-being of society. Yet, governments can also drain community resources and institute flawed policies.

Regardless of how efficiently our government operates, Christ followers are called to submit to governing authorities. Paul tells us that every governing authority has been placed in power by God. Paul doesn't imply that every government official submits to God's lordship or rules virtuously. Rather, Paul teaches that God works through imperfect people in the context of our sinful world. God can use even evil people to accomplish his purposes. Therefore, whether or not our governing authorities rule wisely, we are still commanded to submit to their leadership.

In 1 Timothy, Paul takes his instructions a step further and urges believers to pray for governing authorities. He exhorts, "I urge you, first of all, to pray for all people. Ask God to help them; intercede on their behalf, and give thanks for them. Pray this way for kings and all who are in authority so that we can live peaceful and quiet lives marked by godliness and dignity. This is good and pleases God our Savior, who wants everyone to be saved and to understand the truth," (1 Timothy 2:1–4). Paul instructs us to pray for our leaders, and his reasoning is twofold.

First, we pray for government officials *so that* we can live peacefully under their leadership. Whether or not our leaders know it, our prayers make a difference in their lives. Our prayers can empower them to lead wisely and virtuously. Our prayers can protect them from the deceptive snares of the enemy. Our prayers can make the difference between lives that deteriorate into evil and leaders who govern with integrity. When our authorities lead wisely, we can live peacefully under their rule.

Conversely, if our government becomes evil or calls believers to compromise their faith, we are obligated to disobey (Acts 5:29). When Pharaoh instructed the Hebrew midwives to kill male children, they disobeyed out of reverence for the Lord (Exodus 1:15–17). When King Nebuchadnezzar ordered every person in his kingdom to worship the golden statue of himself, Shadrach, Meshach, and Abednego faced death rather than bow before a false God (Daniel 3:1–30). When Persian officials enacted a law that prohibited prayer to any "god" besides King Darius, Daniel continued his practice of praying to the Lord three times a day (Daniel 6:1–28). Paul, who instructs us to submit to the government, disobeyed his own government numerous times when he was commanded to stop preaching the Gospel.

If we are called to compromise our faith, our loyalty to God takes precedence over government regulations. However, our default attitude should be one of submission. Paul even implies that our peaceful, honorable lives help governing authorities understand the truth of the Gospel, which is his second major point.

We are called to pray for government leaders to incline their hearts toward the Gospel. Paul reminds us that God wants every person to know the truth, and as his children, we should want the same. While our leaders aren't perfect, they are fellow children of God. Let's commit to spend more time praying for our brothers and sisters than complaining about them.

Lord, thank you for moving in the lives of my government officials. I pray that you would fill their minds with your truth and protect them from the deception of the enemy. Incline their hearts toward the Gospel and help them lead with integrity and wisdom. Give them the favor and influence to enact policies that positively impact my community, my state, my country, and my world. Forgive me for speaking disparaging words about those you have placed in positions of authority. Help me see my governing authorities through your eyes and pray for them instead of criticizing them. I ask you to place mentors and supporters around them who will help them grow spiritually and govern effectively. In Jesus' name, Amen

Personal Reflection

Take some time to pray for your state government today. Lift up your governor, lieutenant governor, attorney general, and secretary of state. If you don't know the names of your leaders, look them up so that you can pray for them specifically. Pray that they will accept Christ and grow in their faith. Pray that they will lead wisely with the best interests of the people at heart. Pray that God will guard them from the deception of the enemy and protect them from harm. Pray for your state legislature and ask God to guide them to pass laws that honor him and benefit your state.

Day 7

_____

_____

_____

_____

_____

_____

_____

_____

_____

_____

_____

_____

_____

_____

_____

_____

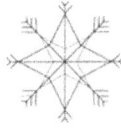

Day 8
Holly Jolly Christmas

The last couple of days we have been talking about the mistletoe plant and the government, both of which can be harmful or helpful depending upon the circumstance. Like mistletoe, holly is another traditional holiday plant with both positives and negatives.

Holly plants are similar to mistletoe plants in that they thrive in cold months. The rich green foliage and bright red berries add color and life to otherwise desolate landscapes during the winter. The berries also serve as a source of food for birds and animals when other forms of sustenance are difficult to find. Even the common belief that holly berries are poisonous to humans is false. The berries and leaves of some species can actually be used to make teas and liquors.

Holly also has plenty of horrible qualities, namely the spiky leaves. Actually, spiky leaves are the only negative, but it's a big one. I despise holly leaves. With more than ten holly bushes in my yard, I get stabbed, scratched, and poked every time I work in my garden. Even worse, when holly leaves fall off a bush and die, they petrify into sharp needles that never seem to decompose.

In sum, holly is a desirable, useful, and beautiful plant, but even holly bushes aren't perfect. Similarly, even the best leaders from among us are still imperfect human beings. Every individual on the earth is influenced by sin. Until sin is finally and decisively dealt with, every single one of our leaders will be imperfect.

Although holly isn't perfect, the plant is traditionally associated with a Savior who is. Holly has a rich symbolic tradition dating back to medieval times. According to tradition, the sharply pointed leaves represent Christ's crown of thorns and the berries represent his blood. The holly plant reminds us that Jesus sacrificed himself and shed his blood to cover our sins.

Centuries prior to the life of Christ, Isaiah anticipated the work of our Savior and his future dominion. He prophesied,

> *For a child is born to us,*
>
> *a son is given to us.*
>
> *The government will rest on his shoulders.*
>
> *And he will be called:*
>
> *Wonderful Counselor, Mighty God,*
>
> *Everlasting Father, Prince of Peace.*
>
> *His government and its peace*
>
> *will never end.*
>
> *He will rule with fairness and justice from the*
>
> *throne of his ancestor David*
>
> *for all eternity.*
>
> ***Isaiah 9:6–7***

When Jesus returns to inaugurate the new heaven and earth, he will reign for eternity. We will no longer struggle to submit to our government because our Savior will rule with perfect fairness and justice. We'll no longer struggle to live in peace because our Lord is the Prince of Peace. In the meantime, we'll eagerly await Jesus' return, trust his sovereignty, and make our world better by praying for our earthly leaders.

Lord, thank you for being born into this sinful earth and living a perfectly sinless life. I look forward to the day when you return to rule all of creation. In the meantime, help me pray for my government with diligence. Help me make my world better by faithfully sharing your love and spreading your Gospel. I ask you to send mature believers to speak into the lives of my governing authorities. Soften their hearts, cause them to be receptive to the Gospel, and help them lead according to your will for this earth. Thank you for hearing and responding to my prayers. In Jesus' name, Amen

Personal Reflection

Take some time to pray for your national government today. Lift up the president and the U.S. cabinet, as well as your state senators and congressional representative(s). If you don't know the names of your leaders, look them up so that you can pray for them specifically. Pray that your government officials will accept Christ and grow in their faith. Pray that they will lead wisely with the best interests of the people at heart. Pray that God will guard them from the deception of the enemy and protect them from harm. Pray that God will help them collaborate in a spirit of harmony rather than division. Pray that God would guide them to implement policies that honor him, benefit your nation, and positively impact the world.

_____

_____

_____

_____

_____

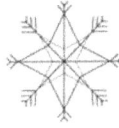

Day 9
Christmas Vacation — Part 1

Let me tell you about one of our most memorable family vacations ever. A few years ago, we traveled to San Antonio the day after Christmas. I had visited the city before, but Wesley and the boys had not. I was excited about introducing them to several unique features of the area, including the nearby town of Fredericksburg. Unfortunately, the entire trip was beset by problems and mishaps, the pinnacle of which was our visit to Fredericksburg.

Fredericksburg is a historical German town in the Texas hill country. My family immigrated to the area several generations ago, and I still have distant relatives in the region. Today, the town has become a bit of a tourist destination, and the traditional Christmas festivities are beautiful.

Fredericksburg is roughly an hour from San Antonio by car, so we took a long ride-share immediately after breakfast. Wesley asked if I was certain we would be able to find a ride back, and I assured him that we would. I reminded him that I'm an experienced traveler and that I've never had trouble finding transportation.

Wesley, Asher, Abel, and I spent an enjoyable day exploring the town. We had a delicious lunch at a trendy restaurant/antique shop. We walked down the central street of the town and visited German-themed shops and Christmas boutiques. Our day concluded with a light display and traditional music in the town square. We had planned to have dinner after the Christmas festivities, but quickly discovered that Fredericksburg shuts down at dusk.

We found ourselves in what felt like a Twilight Zone episode. Within minutes, all the lights turned off, the shops locked up, and the people disappeared. We realized that we wouldn't find dinner nearby, so we began searching for a ride back to San Antonio. As the minutes ticked by and we continued to search, I began to regret my confident assurances from the morning. Despite my certainty that we would find a ride back, we most certainly did not.

I'll finish the story tomorrow, but let me pause to make a point. According to Proverbs 13:16, "Wise people think before they act; fools don't—and even brag about their foolishness." Instead of planning ahead to ensure my family would have transportation at the end of the day, I bragged about my traveling experience. I behaved foolishly and our whole family faced the consequences.

Forethought and planning can stave off potential pitfalls and distress. Consider your course of action before you run headlong into the unknown. Take preemptive steps to avoid obstacles instead of dashing into a brick wall.

I hope you can learn from my foolish mistake. Plan ahead and you'll save yourself time, resources, and heartache. You may also save those closest to you from experiencing the disaster you caused.

Lord, thank you for providing me with the capacity for forethought and planning. Help me think before I act and make wise decisions. Prevent me from encountering mishaps and obstacles. Help me humbly submit to your guidance and seek your ways. Let me be an example of wisdom rather than folly to the people you've placed in my life. In Jesus' name, Amen

Personal Reflection

Take time for self-evaluation. Do you tend to plan wisely, over plan, or not plan at all? Do you proactively think before you act or impulsively rush from one opportunity to the next? Do you tend to plan well in one area of your life while omitting other areas? Consider your spiritual life, your relational life, and your professional life (if applicable). Think of one way you can be more proactive or use more forethought in each area.

_____

_____

_____

_____

_____

_____

_____

_____

_____

_____

_____

_____

Day 9

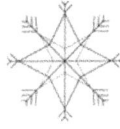

Day 10
Christmas Vacation — Part 2

Yesterday, I began telling you about our vacation in San Antonio and our day in Fredericksburg. Although I was certain that we would be able to find an Uber back to San Antonio at the end of the day, we couldn't. As we stood in the town square, we placed panicked requests for transportation over and over on our phones. (Pro tip: Repeatedly and frantically requesting rides does not increase your likelihood of securing one.) We finally gave up and decided that our best course of action would be to find a place to stay overnight.

To our immense relief, we found a cheap hotel less than a mile down the road. We quickly made our way to the hotel and requested a room for the night. To our surprise, our credit card was declined. What we hadn't realized was that each ride request we'd made over the last hour had created a pending charge on our credit card. In our panic, we had requested so many rides that our credit card had been suspected stolen and placed in suspension.

Although our panicked behavior caused a potential catastrophe, God's grace saved the day. I happened to have an extra, unused credit card in my wallet that I'd activated simply to earn airline miles. With my airline card, we were able to book a room without further hindrance. Then, the hotel receptionist provided contact info for a local driver who was willing to take us home first thing in the morning. The receptionist also provided toiletries and loaned us phone chargers. God, in his providence, had already provided solutions to our problems.

We trusted God throughout the ordeal, but I would be lying if I said we didn't have moments of panic. At points, I worried that my stupidity was going to result in my children sleeping on the street. Yet, each time panic swelled, I took fear captive and submitted it to faith. We prayed as a family and calmly sought God's guidance.

As promised, our Father provided what we needed at each step and even blessed us with a memorable night of bonding. I can confidently say that I believe Paul's encouragement that "[God] will supply all your needs from his glorious riches, which have been given to us in Christ Jesus," (Philippians 4:19). I hope you'll place faith in that promise as well.

Lord, thank you for meeting all my needs. I believe that you have the power and resources to protect me and provide for me. Help me trust you more so that worry can't consume my mind and heart. Help me learn strategies for staying calm and making wise decisions in the midst of challenging circumstances. Give me the opportunity to be a peaceful influence on others who might be struggling with anxiety or fear. Thank you for going ahead of me to create solutions to problems I don't anticipate. Thank you for helping me and loving me even when I'm the source of the problem. In Jesus' name, Amen

Personal Reflection

Read Philippians 4 in entirety. Write down every strategy for living in peace and contentment that you can find.

Scan the QR code for passages of Scripture

_____

_____

_____

_____

_____

_____

_____

_____

_____

_____

_____

_____

_____

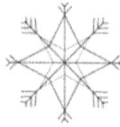

Day 11
Terrible, No Good, Horrible, Very Bad Days for King Hezekiah

The last couple of days, I've talked about our unintentional sleep-over in Fredericksburg. My pride and foolishness caused the initial problem, which was our inability to find an Uber. Our panic was the root of our second mistake, in which we frantically requested rides until our credit card was suspended. Ultimately, we were fine, but our poor planning and panicked reaction could have caused a disaster. If we had planned wisely, we wouldn't have gotten stuck in the first place. If we hadn't panicked, our credit card wouldn't have been cut off in the middle of our vacation.

Poor planning and panicked reactions never lead to pleasant outcomes. In Scripture, King Zedekiah could serve as the poster child for this principle. From the start of his reign, the threat of Babylonian occupation loomed. Seeking a way to avoid calamity, Zedekiah sought the advice of Jeremiah the prophet.

> Jeremiah said to Zedekiah, "This is what the Lord God of Heaven's Armies, the God of Israel, says: 'If you surrender to the Babylonian officers, you and your family will live, and the city will not be burned down. But if you refuse to surrender, you will not escape! This city will be handed over to the Babylonians, and they will burn it to the ground.'" "But I am afraid to surrender," the king said, "for the

Babylonians may hand me over to the Judeans who have defected to them. And who knows what they will do to me!" Jeremiah replied, "You won't be handed over to them if you choose to obey the Lord. Your life will be spared, and all will go well for you"
Jeremiah 38:17–20

Jeremiah advised King Zedekiah to surrender. The prophet knew God had already declared that Babylon would be the instrument with which he would punish Judah's unfaithfulness (Jeremiah 25:8–11). Yet, Zedekiah resisted Jeremiah's advice and rejected God. Accordingly, Zedekiah faced the consequences of his choice.

When King Zedekiah of Judah and all the soldiers saw that the Babylonians had broken into the city, they fled. They waited for nightfall and then slipped through the gate between the two walls behind the king's garden and headed toward the Jordan Valley. But the Babylonian troops chased them and overtook Zedekiah on the plains of Jericho. They captured him and took him to King Nebuchadnezzar of Babylon, who was at Riblah in the land of Hamath. There the king of Babylon pronounced judgment upon Zedekiah. The king of Babylon made Zedekiah watch as he slaughtered his sons at Riblah. The king of Babylon also slaughtered all the nobles of Judah. Then he gouged out Zedekiah's eyes and bound him in bronze chains to lead him away to Babylon.
Jeremiah 39:4–7

If Zedekiah had faithfully submitted to God's will, he could have spared himself, his sons, his advisors, and his people. Instead, he allowed fear to fill his heart. Rather than trusting God and taking steps to mediate the damage of the invasion, he cowered in his palace. Zedekiah's panic paralyzed him until the Babylonians were on his doorstep and his only recourse was a futile attempt to flee.

Zedekiah's story is one of the most tragic in Scripture. The narrative is so horrible that I'm uncomfortable even writing about it. Yet, we can learn a vital lesson from Zedekiah. Fear is not our friend and panic does facilitate wise planning. In fact, "God has not given us a spirit of fear and timidity, but of power, love, and self-discipline," (2 Timothy 1:7). God has already equipped us to overcome every circumstance. We don't cower in fear, we conquer with love.

Next time you are in a trial, self-inflicted or otherwise, take time to ground yourself in God's love and trust that he will help you (Proverbs 3:5–6). Draw upon self-discipline to calm your mind and your body. Access his power through prayer and ask for wisdom. Then you can begin to plan, prepare, and proceed with confident faith.

Lord, thank you for providing power, love and self-discipline, through which I can conquer any fear. Teach me to seek your wisdom in scary situations rather than behaving rashly or becoming paralyzed by anxiety. Help me make decisions based on faith rather than fear. Help me remain courageous and calm in every circumstance. I pray that my life would be a peaceful influence on those around me. Give me the opportunity to encourage others with my example of abiding trust in you. In Jesus' name, Amen

Personal Reflection

Yesterday we talked about strategies for maintaining peace in the mist of challenging circumstances. Today we'll add another strategy to our toolbox—the practice of grounding. Grounding can help take your mind off of anxious thoughts, calm your body, and soothe chaotic emotions. One common grounding technique is the 5-4-3-2-1 method. As you breathe slowly and deeply, notice five things you can see, four things you can feel, three things you can hear, two things you can smell, and one thing you can taste. Take a moment now to try out this technique, then practice it several times throughout your day.

_____

_____

_____

_____

_____

_____

_____

_____

_____

_____

_____

_____

_____

_____

Day 12
Making Memories

The last few days, I've talked about our vacation in San Antonio and our trip to Fredericksburg. The whole trip was beset by problems to the point that our catchphrase became "making memories." In other words, the only positive thing we could say was that the trip was unforgettable.

The phrase "making memories" represented our determination to make the best of each experience, whether good, bad or ugly. When I got us stuck in Fredericksburg, Wesley and the boys could have been furious with me. Instead, they offered grace and forgave my mistake. We could have been angry with God for not sending a ride home and letting our credit card get declined. Instead, we thanked him for the nearby hotel and a back-up credit card. We could have sulked over the convenience store food we had to eat for dinner. Instead, we thanked God for providing a convenience store that was still open. We could have grumbled at having to sleep in a ratty hotel in Fredericksburg while simultaneously paying for a nice condo in San Antonio. Instead, we were thankful that we found a room at all. We could have complained about the disgusting brown bathtub. Instead, we laughed and committed to solidarity in skipping showers. We could have spent the night bemoaning our misfortune. Instead, we ate gas station popcorn, watched a movie on the tiny TV, and relished our time together. What started out as a disaster has now turned into one of our fondest memories.

Before I close the San Antonio saga, let me share one more note-worthy memory. On the final evening of our trip, we wanted ice cream after dinner. Through an internet search, we located a shop within walking distance and plugged the address into the phone GPS

The temperature was becoming uncomfortably cold, but we decided to walk since the shop was nearby. As we walked, however, the streets became darker and more deserted, and the ice cream shop didn't seem to be getting any closer. We soon realized that the GPS had malfunctioned and led us to an unsavory part of town. Even worse, we were completely lost. As we walked down a dark street full of boarded up tenements, I shakily laughed and said "making memories." From a nearby dark alley, we heard a slurred male voice repeat "making memories." In near hysterical laughter, we increased our pace to a jog and prayed that no one was chasing us.

A few minutes later, Abel slowed down for a conversation with a new friend. We hadn't even realized he had stopped until we were across the street from Abel and his "friend." We furiously waved for him to cut off the conversation and catch up. Abel, refusing to join us, yelled across the street, "She just needs a dollar." Suffice to say, Wesley grabbed our son and we quickly left the scene. Thankfully, we soon made it back to civilization. Despite our mishap, we emerged un-scathed, and we did indeed make lots of memories.

Although some of our memories were scary, we made the best of a rough vacation and we can now laugh about it freely. The Apostle Paul also understood how to be content in the face of difficulties and disappointments. In Philippians 4, Paul explains:

Don't worry about anything; instead, pray about everything. Tell God what you need, and thank him for all he has done. Then you will experience God's peace, which exceeds anything we can understand. His peace

*will guard your hearts and minds as you live in Christ
Jesus . . . I know how to live on almost nothing or
with everything. I have learned the secret of living in
every situation, whether it is with a full stomach or
empty, with plenty or little. For I can do everything
through Christ, who gives me strength.*

Philippians 4:6–7, 12–13

When our lives are rooted in prayer, gratitude, and faith, our minds can remain at peace in any circumstance. Because our hearts are full of his love, frustration, anger, and fear have no room to take root.

Lord, Grow my faith and shrink my fear. Fill my heart with peace so great that worry has no room to grow. Help me see the best in every situation rather than seeing only the negative. When I encounter difficult situations, help me remember to pray, give thanks, and trust in your strength. In Jesus' name, Amen

Personal Reflection

Review the strategies for living in peace and contentment from the last two days. Choose one to practice throughout your day today.

_____

_____

_____

_____

_____

_____

Day 13
Good Gifts

I have an adorable niece and nephew. My six-year-old niece, Lilly, is a girly girl. She loves dresses and jewelry and shoes and anything pink. My nephew, Dylan, is an energetic, rowdy ten-year-old.

A little while back, my sister purchased each of them a surprise gift. She bought a delicate pink bracelet for Lilly and a dolphin stuffed animal for Dylan. I expected Lilly to be delighted by her new bracelet since she loves jewelry and all things pink, but she was not. She wailed, "Dylan got a big present, and I got a little present!"

Lilly's disappointment wasn't actually caused by her gift. Lilly's bracelet was perfect for *her*, and Dylan's dolphin was perfect for *him*. Neither gift was better, and neither gift was more valuable—they were simply different. Yet, Lilly became upset when she compared her gift to Dylan's. When Lilly looked at Dylan's stuffed animal, her bracelet seemed inferior by comparison.

You and I often react similarly to the gifts that God gives us. We compare our spiritual gifts, our possessions, our homes, our job titles, and even our physical appearances. Although our gifts are special blessings from God, they can seem inferior when we compare them with the gifts of others.

I remember when Wesley and I purchased our first home. I was so joyful and full of gratitude. I thought our new home was beautiful and spacious . . . until a friend invited me to her new home, which was newer, nicer, and twice the size of mine. All of a sudden, my own home seemed small and shabby in comparison. Yet, nothing had changed except my perspective. My home was perfect for my little family, which at that time consisted of myself, Wesley, and baby Asher. Only when I compared my home with my friend's home did it seem inadequate.

Comparison is the enemy of contentment. If you view life through the lens of comparison, you'll always be able to identify someone with more skills, education, influence, money, or beauty. However, God has provided each of us with wonderful gifts. In fact, John tells us that "From [God's] abundance we have all received one gracious blessing after another," (John 1:16). His blessings for me are tailor made for *me*, and his blessings for you are tailor made for *you*. Let's replace comparison with celebration today.

Lord, thank you for the abundant gifts and blessings you've showered upon me. Help me grow in gratitude so that I'm not tempted to compare my gifts. Teach me to celebrate the gifts and blessings of others instead of coveting them. Give me a greater measure of contentment and joy as I serve you with the resources you've provided. Give me wisdom as I seek to use my gifts for the benefit of your kingdom and the betterment of our world. In Jesus' name, Amen

Personal Reflection

Review the blessings that you listed on Day 1. Thank God afresh and continue the list below. Write down your spiritual gifts, personal strengths, material resources, and any fresh blessings for which you are thankful. Each time you are tempted to feel resentment or jealousy over the gifts of others today, remind yourself how abundantly God has blessed you!

Day 13

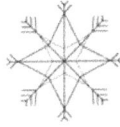

Day 14
Christmas Cheer

Yesterday we talked about the good gifts God showers upon each of us. Today we'll continue discussing our gifts. More specifically, we'll talk about how God blesses us with gifts as well as opportunities to use them.

Our Father generously shares gifts with us so we can share them with others. Peter encourages, "Cheerfully share your home with those who need a meal or a place to stay. God has given each of you a gift from his great variety of spiritual gifts. Use them well to serve one another," (1 Peter 4:9–10). The apostle encourages us to use both spiritual gifts and material blessings to serve God and others.

For those of us who are Christ followers, service should be a foundational part of our lives. Paul explains that we were, in fact, created for the *purpose* of serving others (Ephesians 2:10). Even Jesus didn't come to be served, but to serve (Mark 10:45). So, not only do we become like our Savior when we serve, but we also find purpose and fulfillment.

Even better, our loving Father has prepared good works for each of us in advance (Ephesians 2:10). These opportunities to serve aren't burdensome, like the lists of chores I give my teenage boys. Rather, the opportunities for service that God prepares for us, when undertaken with the right heart, result in greater joy and blessing in our own lives.

For example, I love to serve my family, especially during the holidays. Throughout the month of December, I surprise the boys with small gifts, such as decorations for their rooms or holiday pajamas. I make time to prepare Wesley's favorite meals, like fried chicken and homemade pot-pie. I plan cheerful holiday activities for the whole family. I create entertaining scenes with our elf-on-the-shelf, even though my boys are long past the age where they believe our elf, Smiley, is real.

I regard serving my family as a blessing, not a burden. Nonetheless, there are sacrificial elements of my holiday service. I must strictly budget my time and money. I must give up some things that I enjoy, like extra workout time and fancy coffee. Not every aspect of every act of service is fun, but the end result—joy and fulfillment—makes the sacrifices worthwhile. Although I'm extra busy, and sometimes even stressed-out, I treasure the Christmas cheer my service brings to my family.

Serving God likewise requires an element of sacrifice. Sometimes I would rather be at home sitting by a cozy fire than serving at a chilly community outreach. Sometimes I would rather sleep late on a Sunday morning than get up early for church. However, the opportunity to share Jesus with the world and minister to his people yields blessings that outweigh any sacrifice.

Serving God doesn't solely refer to a church context either. Serving our families and friends *is* serving God. Showing Christ's love in our workplace or offering kind words to strangers *is* serving God. When you share the gifts of your Father, your blessings never run out, and your joy will outweigh your sacrifice. Let's spread some Christmas cheer by serving our Lord, sharing his love, and serving others.

Lord, thank you for providing opportunities for me to serve you and for equipping me with everything I need to carry out the good works that you have prepared for me. Help me to serve you with humility and selflessness. Help me to reflect your selfless sacrifice as I serve my family, my coworkers, my friends, and my church. Please expose any wrong attitudes toward service I might be harboring in my heart. Help me serve with the motivation of pleasing you, building your kingdom, and loving others well. Help me be attentive to the needs of those around me and help me be aware of opportunities to serve you. Thank you for the opportunity and blessing of serving you. In Jesus' name, Amen

Personal Reflection

Take time to prayerfully evaluate your attitude toward service. Meditate on the following questions and write down at least two ways you can grow in your attitude toward serving or your practice of service.

- Is serving God and other people a fundamental part of your life?
- Do you serve with joy or do you serve out of obligation?
- Are you willing to perform acts of service for which you will receive no attention or recognition?
- Do you sacrificially give of your time, talent, and resources or do you only serve when convenient?
- How can you better serve God through serving your family, friends, and/or church?

_____

_____

_____

_____

_____

Day 14

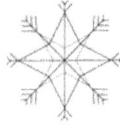

Day 15
Birthday Dinner — Part 1

My birthday is in December, so birthday celebrations are part of our holiday festivities. One year, Wesley decided he wanted to cook dinner for me. I was apprehensive, and let me explain why.

In our household, we all share domestic responsibilities. We all clean, do laundry, care for the dogs, and maintain the yard. However, we don't all cook. I've always enjoyed cooking, so I've always been the one to prepare meals. As the boys grew up, they learned to cook alongside me. Now that my boys are older, they share the cooking responsibilities. Wesley isn't unwilling to cook; he has just never had a reason to learn.

Therefore, when Wesley expressed his desire to cook my birthday dinner, my concern was legitimate. Yet, my husband is a smart and capable man, so I reasoned that if he was confident, I could trust him to prepare a simple meal. Unfortunately, Wesley chose a recipe that was far too complex for his basic cooking skills. I'll finish the story tomorrow, but let me pause here to make a point and tell you that Wesley's foray into cooking did not go well.

You and I are also prone to miscalculate our skills and abilities at times. Perhaps we feel like we are ready for the next level of responsibility in our ministry or our workplace. We might even feel like we deserve a more noteworthy job or more visible ministry role. Perhaps we think we have earned more respect and influence than we've been given.

We might actually have the skills and maturity needed for the next level. More often, though, if we aren't receiving the advancement we desire, our earthly leaders and our Heavenly Father are holding us back for a reason. Typically, when God holds us back, he is protecting us. When we overestimate our skills and attempt a task for which we are unprepared, we can create a huge mess for ourselves and the people around us.

Fortunately, Paul offers a strategy for preventing messy disasters. He instructs, "Don't think you are better than you really are. Be honest in your evaluation of yourselves, measuring yourselves by the faith God has given us," (Romans 12:3b). Paul advises us to engage in honest self-assessment: What are our strengths and weaknesses? Under what circumstances do we thrive and under what conditions do we struggle?

At the same time, Paul also encourages us to measure ourselves through the rubric of faith. When we accept Christ, our faith should change the way we think. We no longer measure our worth by the standards of the world. Our strengths aren't ranked according to ones that will garner more income, success, or fame. Further, our perceived weaknesses are opportunities for God to work in our lives. In sum, we self-assess through the lens of God's priorities, not those of the world.

When we accurately self-assess we not only prevent a messy disaster, but we serve God more effectively. Instead of being angry over unmet expectations or disappointed by failed endeavors, we can walk in our purpose with contentment and serve God with joy.

Lord, thank you in advance for helping me honestly assess my personal strengths and opportunities for growth. Show me how to evaluate myself in the light of my faith and your Word. I pray that you would be glorified as I patiently grow in spiritual giftings, personal maturity, and professional competency. Help me live in humility as I serve you and your people. Give me the courage to embrace new challenges and the wisdom to seek guidance. In Jesus' Name, Amen

Personal Reflection

Prayerfully take a few minutes to self-assess right now. First, make a list of at least ten strengths and skills. Include spiritual gifts, professional skills, relational strengths, or any other areas of personal gifting. Second, make a list of at least ten opportunities for growth. Include spiritual, professional, and relational areas in which you would like to develop further. Finally, thank God for the items on each list, and ask him to reveal which strengths and opportunities he would like you to develop further.

_____

_____

_____

_____

_____

_____

_____

_____

Day 15

_____

_____

_____

_____

_____

_____

_____

_____

_____

_____

_____

_____

_____

_____

_____

_____

_____

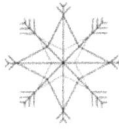

Day 16
Birthday Dinner — Part 2

Yesterday we talked about Wesley's unsuccessful attempt to cook my birthday dinner. Although I was apprehensive, I trusted him to assess his own cooking skills and choose an appropriate recipe. As you already know, Wesley chose a recipe for which his cooking skills were inadequate.

On the evening of my birthday, I was enjoying an extended workout while Wesley cooked dinner. The first warning that dinner was not going as planned was a burnt smell emanating from the kitchen. I yelled across the house to ask if Wesley needed help, but he assured me that everything was fine. Against my better judgment, I continued exercising. The second warning that dinner prep was going poorly was a cloud of smoke that began seeping through the house.

I immediately rushed to the kitchen, where Wesley was burning chicken and—totally unaware—seconds away from a grease fire. I immediately removed the food from the stovetop and turned off the stove. We opened doors and windows to circulate fresh air and placed the burned pan of grease outside.

With the disaster under control, I helped Wesley salvage most of the food. Dinner was served later than planned, but we still had a lovely family meal. The food turned out fine, and I enjoyed celebrating my birthday with my family. However, Wesley felt disappointed and frustrated at his perceived failure.

Yesterday, we talked about how honest self-assessment can prevent messy situations and disappointments in our lives. We often desire promotion, influence, and greater responsibility. We may think we are ready to fly, then take a big leap and crash to the ground. Although we can learn from mistakes and failures, God will often help us avoid them altogether.

So, how can we ensure that we are ready for our next step? First, we can honestly self-assess, as we talked about yesterday. Second, we can humbly learn from leaders who are more mature, skilled, and experienced. Peter advises, "you who are younger must accept the authority of the elders. And all of you, dress yourselves in humility as you relate to one another, for "God opposes the proud but gives grace to the humble." So humble yourselves under the mighty power of God, and at the right time he will lift you up in honor," (1 Peter 5:5–6).

God places people in our lives to help us grow in our gifts, skills, and spiritual maturity. More mature brothers and sisters in Christ can help us accurately assess our strengths and opportunities for growth. Wise leaders can help us identify our gifts, provide constructive feedback, and guide us in the right direction. They can help us develop our gifts and provide resources for further equipping. They can help us grow spiritually and learn to rely on God rather than our skills. They'll provide opportunities for growth while ministering alongside us. They'll catch us if we fall and help us learn from our mistakes. Yet, we must allow them to speak into our lives. Just as Wesley should have let me help him cook dinner before he attempted an entire meal on his own, we must learn from the people God places in our lives.

The key to growth is a humble and teachable spirit. As we follow our leaders and submit to their guidance, we are encouraged, strengthened, and equipped. If we follow in the humble example of Christ, God provides growth and promotion at just the right time.

Lord, thank you for preparing me to serve you well. Give me patience and humility in abundance so that I can grow in my skills and my spiritual maturity. Help me always remember that you are the source of my strength and the giver of every gift. I pray that my service would bring glory to you and that I would never seek acclaim for myself. Help me submit to my leaders and learn from them. Reveal specific individuals from whom I can learn. I pray that you would supernaturally multiply my efforts so that I accomplish much on your behalf. In Jesus' name, Amen

Personal Reflection

Prayerfully review the lists of strengths and opportunities you created yesterday. First, ask God to show you how you can use at least one of your strengths more effectively or how he would have you develop it further. Second, ask God to reveal at least one item from your growth opportunity list that he would like you to strengthen. Third, consider talking with a pastor, leader, or mentor to help you self-evaluate and suggest strategies for growth.

Day 16

Day 17
Empty Stocking

Today I'm going to share Wesley's kryptonite—gift giving. Despite all his strengths as a husband, he struggles to plan ahead for special events. He is very pragmatic and frugal by nature, so giving and receiving gifts is not a high priority in his life. Fortunately, I don't need spectacular gifts to feel loved, but I do need to feel acknowledged on special occasions. I've had to help Wesley to grow in this area.

For years after we got married, I filled Wesley's Christmas stocking to overflowing while mine sat empty. After the boys were born, I filled three stockings every Christmas while mine remained sad and limp. I was hesitant to seem negative or ungrateful on Christmas, so I stayed silent each year.

As I've grown in Christ, I've learned to err on the side of caution and hold my tongue. Because my natural instinct is to be overly direct, keeping my mouth shut is usually the safest option. Yet, the counsel of Scripture can be confusing about when to speak and when to remain silent. For example, look at these verses from Proverbs 26.

Don't answer the foolish arguments of fools,
or you will become as foolish as they are.
Be sure to answer the foolish arguments of fools,
or they will become wise in their own estimation.
Proverbs 26:4–5

What we can learn from these contradictory proverbs is that each situation requires discernment. Sometimes we should remain silent, but sometimes the wise course of action is to speak out.

I thus decided that my resentful feelings at Christmas were not healthy for myself or my marriage. One Christmas morning, after another disappointment, I spoke with Wesley. I waited until we were done opening presents and the boys were engaged with their gifts. Once we were alone, I simply told Wesley that I would enjoy stocking stuffers next year. We didn't have a blowout, I didn't speak in anger, and Wesley didn't get defensive. He hadn't even realized I was disappointed and was happy I shared my feelings.

Because Wesley and I communicated honestly, calmly, and clearly, we were able to stave off potential discord in the future and safeguard the continuing health of our relationship. Proverbs 25 addresses the value of honest, open feedback.

> *Timely advice is lovely,*
> *like golden apples in a silver basket.*
> *To one who listens, valid criticism*
> *is like a gold earring or other gold jewelry.*
> ### *Proverbs 25:11–12*

The verses point out key elements in productive dialogue. First, the speaker should offer advice in the right circumstance. In other words, criticizing Wesley in front of the boys while we were opening presents would not have been a good time and place. Second, the feedback must be valid. Words spoken with the intent to harm or belittle only create further conflict. Third, the hearer must listen to the advice and acknowledge its validity.

Although we don't have the power to change someone else's heart, the way we present advice, criticism, or feedback goes a long way toward a positive reception. Let's set ourselves up for success in every communication and speak wise words at the right time.

Lord, thank you for teaching me to communicate in a loving and timely manner. Give me the wisdom to know when constructive feedback is appropriate and when it's better to hold my tongue. Help me also to humbly accept productive feedback from others. Grow my capacity for self-awareness and self-control so that I never speak with the intent to wound. Fill my heart with such great love for other people that I communicate only with pure motives. In Jesus' name, Amen

Personal Reflection

Seek opportunities to give and receive feedback today. Notice how you respond to constructive criticism from others. Do you seek to learn from feedback or do you tend to become defensive. Also be aware of your tendencies in regard to giving feedback. Do you prayerfully seek appropriate opportunities for offering feedback, do you avoid confrontation, or do you bluntly share your opinion whenever you feel the urge?

_____

_____

_____

_____

_____

_____

Day 17

_____

_____

_____

_____

_____

_____

_____

_____

_____

_____

_____

_____

_____

_____

_____

_____

_____

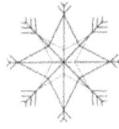

Day 18
What Child Is This? — Part 1

In this season of Christ's birth, I sometimes reminisce on the birth of my own two babies. The birth of each little boy was the beginning of an exciting journey full of new blessings and opportunities. Yet, their births were also the culmination of many months of preparation. Before the boys were born, Wesley and I converted a spare bedroom to a nursery and purchased all the requisite baby supplies. I visited the doctor countless times and underwent a battery of prenatal tests.

Similarly, the birth of Christ was the beginning of something new, but also the culmination of much planning and preparation on the part of our Heavenly Father. Jesus' advent, or arrival, inaugurated a new era of salvation history, but it was also an event God had been planning for millennia.

In the opening chapters of Scripture, God foreshadows his plan to restore the fractured relationship between himself and humanity. Speaking to the Serpent and to Eve, he says, "I will cause hostility between you and the woman, and between your offspring and her offspring. He will strike your head, and you will strike his heel," (Genesis 3:15).

As part of God's curse upon the Serpent, he promises that a descendant of Eve will one day deliver a fatal blow to the enemy. God later reaffirms his promise with Abraham and David, and through them the children of Israel. As the centuries passed, every faithful

Jewish man and woman, boy and girl, lived in eager anticipation of the fulfillment of God's promise, the advent of the Messiah.

When the angel of the Lord spoke to Mary, she would have understood his message. She listened as he announced:

> *"You will conceive and give birth to a son, and you will name him Jesus. He will be very great and will be called the Son of the Most High. The Lord God will give him the throne of his ancestor David. And he will reign over Israel forever; his Kingdom will never end!"*
>
> *... Mary responded, "I am the Lord's servant. May everything you have said about me come true." And then the angel left her.*

> ### *Luke 1:31–33, 38*

The angel informed Mary that she would bear a son named Jesus—translated "Salvation" in Hebrew—who would reign forever. As the gravity of the angel's message became clear, Mary responded in faith. Despite the shocking news, Mary calmly submitted to the Lord's will.

Although Mary was surprised by the angel's message, she wasn't unprepared. Her time spent in the study of Scripture had equipped her to understand God's plan. Her moments spent in prayer had empowered her to respond in faith. Her lifestyle of obedience had equipped her to serve the Lord when he called.

Our lives are full of surprises. Some of them are wonderful and some of them are not so wonderful. None of them are a surprise to God. Even now he is making preparations to protect, provide, and equip you to succeed. We must likewise prepare ourselves so that when the moment comes, we can respond, like Mary, with fortitude and faith.

Lord, Thank you for moving on my behalf, even when I can't see your hand at work. Help me be diligent to prepare and equip myself for whatever my future holds. Give me the discipline to study, pray, and serve faithfully. Empower me to resist every temptation of the enemy that might weaken my faith and disrupt my relationship with you. Grow my faith so that I am prepared to follow you down every path, even unexpected ones. I pray that my faith and obedience would be an inspiration to others. In Jesus' name, Amen

Personal Reflection

Prayerfully reflect on unexpected events in your past. Ask God how you could have better prepared yourself and how you could have responded more faithfully. Write down your thoughts. We'll revisit them tomorrow.

_____

_____

_____

_____

_____

_____

_____

_____

_____

_____

Day 18

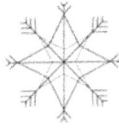

Day 19
What Child Is This? — Part 2

Yesterday we talked about the birth of Christ. Although God was inaugurating a new era of history, the advent of Jesus had been part of God's plan from the very beginning. The author of Genesis describes the deception of Eve by Satan and reveals God's plan of redemption. God promises a future descendant who will defeat the deceiver.

In Revelation, John expands upon the cosmic battle taking place on earth.

> *Then I witnessed in heaven an event of great significance. I saw a woman clothed with the sun, with the moon beneath her feet, and a crown of twelve stars on her head. She was pregnant, and she cried out because of her labor pains and the agony of giving birth. . . . [The dragon] stood in front of the woman as she was about to give birth, ready to devour her baby as soon as it was born. She gave birth to a son who was to rule all nations with an iron rod. And her child was snatched away from the dragon and was caught up to God and to his throne. And the woman fled into the wilderness, where God had prepared a place to care for her for 1,260 days.*
>
> *Revelation 12:1–2, 4–6*

The woman represents Eve, Israel, and Mary, all in one. In her persona and her progeny, God's redemptive promises converge. Similarly, the dragon embodies Satan's perennial war against God's people. However, the dragon is neither able to destroy the woman nor her offspring.

In the subsequent verses, John describes the same events from a heavenly perspective. As the earthly battle rages between God's people and the forces of the enemy in 12:1–6, a heavenly battle simultaneously takes place, as described in 12:7–9.

> *Then there was war in heaven. Michael and his angels fought against the dragon and his angels. And the dragon lost the battle, and he and his angels were forced out of heaven. This great dragon—the ancient serpent called the devil, or Satan, the one deceiving the whole world—was thrown down to the earth with all his angels.*
>
> ***Revelation 12:7–9***

As Jesus was crucified, God's angels fought Satan and his demonic legions in the supernatural realm. Although the death of the Messiah looked like defeat, it was actually the prerequisite to his triumph. When Christ was resurrected, death was defeated. Then, as the Lord ascended, Satan was cast down.

> *Then I heard a loud voice shouting across the heavens, "It has come at last—salvation and power and the Kingdom of our God, and the authority of his Christ. For the accuser of our brothers and sisters has been thrown down to earth—the one who accuses them before our God day and night. And they have defeated*

him by the blood of the Lamb and by their testimony."
Revelation 12:10-11

Although Satan and his demons are temporarily free to roam the earth, they have already been defeated. Satan has been overcome by the blood of the lamb and the power of the Gospel message. At the cross, Jesus struck the final blow of the war. Now, the enemy and his forces fight from a position of defeat. Yet, as long as we walk in the truth of the Gospel, we walk as victors. We can reject the lies of the enemy because we know the truth.

This season, as we celebrate the birth of Jesus, let's remember to thank him for his sacrificial death. Even better, let's honor his sacrifice by walking in the power of his victory.

Lord, thank you for fighting on my behalf, defeating the enemy, and winning the victory for me. Show me areas of my life in which I'm allowing the enemy to deceive me. Reveal any patterns of thought or behaviors in which I'm allowing the enemy to have influence. Help me to daily walk in victory and boldly confess the truth of the Gospel. Help me seek opportunities to share the Gospel so that others can be freed from the deception of the enemy and walk in your truth. In Jesus' name, Amen

Personal Reflection

Yesterday, I asked you to reflect on unexpected events in your past and ask God how you could have responded more faithfully. Re-read what you wrote down and add any additional thoughts you might have today. Next, meditate on the following: Can you think of any unexpected moments that felt like defeat, but actually ended up becoming a blessing? Perhaps the end of one relationship opened the door to a healthier one. Perhaps God allowed you to lose your job so he could give you a better position. Once again, ask God what you

can learn from these past surprises or disappointments so that you
can respond more faithfully and wisely in the future.

_____

_____

_____

_____

_____

_____

_____

_____

_____

_____

_____

_____

_____

_____

_____

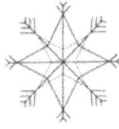

Day 20
Angels We Have Heard on High

During the Christmas season, we see images of beautiful angels everywhere. These luminous beings are portrayed with flowing robes, snowy wings, lustrous hair, and a gentle smile. Due to my snarky disposition, I always snort and roll my eyes when I see images of the lovely figures. I can't help but snicker at the thought of replacing the human-like figures with biblically accurate angels.

Have you ever noticed that angels evoke extreme fear when they encounter individuals in the Bible? In Luke 1–2 alone, angelic beings evoke fear on three separate occasions. When Gabriel appears to Zechariah to announce the birth of John the Baptist, the priest is "shaken and overwhelmed with fear" (Luke 1:12). When Gabriel appears to Mary, she is confused, disturbed, and afraid (Luke 1:29–30). When an angel appears to the shepherds, they are terrified (Luke 2:9).

Their fear isn't simply due to the angels' holy radiance. Based on description in Scripture, angels, in fact, often look terrifying. The angelic creatures in Ezekiel are a psychedelic amalgamation of human and animal parts. The prophet records,

> *[The creatures] looked human, ⁶ except that each had four faces and four wings. Their legs were straight, and their feet had hooves like those of a calf and shone like burnished bronze. Under each of their four wings I could see human hands. So each of the four beings*

> *had four faces and four wings. . . . Each had a human face in the front, the face of a lion on the right side, the face of an ox on the left side, and the face of an eagle at the back.*
>
> **Ezekiel 1:5–8, 10**

A few decades after Ezekiel's encounter, Daniel sees a different being that is nearly as alarming as Ezekiel's creatures.

> *I looked up and saw a man dressed in linen clothing, with a belt of pure gold around his waist. His body looked like a precious gem. His face flashed like lightning, and his eyes flamed like torches. His arms and feet shone like polished bronze, and his voice roared like a vast multitude of people.*
>
> **Daniel 10:5–6**

While some angels are bizarre and frightful in appearance, they can also appear perfectly human. In Genesis 18, Abraham dines with three "men" before realizing they are angelic messengers from God. In Hebrews 13:2, we are exhorted to show hospitality to strangers as they might be angels in disguise. It, thus, appears that angels may have the ability to alter their form and appearance as needed.

So, what relevance do angels have for our lives? Why are we discussing these powerful, shimmering, possibly shape-shifting entities? First, I want to drive home the reality that angels are fearsome beings. Angels aren't innocuous little cherubs who lounge in the clouds and play harps. Angels are powerful warriors of God, as you saw in the verses from yesterday.

Second, I want to point out that God has charged his angels with protecting you! According to Psalm 91:11–12, "[The Lord] will order his angels to protect you wherever you go. They will hold you up with their hands so you won't even hurt your foot on a stone." God's fearsome warriors surround us and protect us everywhere we go! We don't face our fears and trials alone. Next time you feel overwhelmed, afraid, or defeated, remember that God's powerful angels are fighting on your behalf.

Lord, thank you for sending your warriors to fight on my behalf. I pray that my faith would grow so strong that fear would not be able to take root in my heart. Help me release my worries to you and trust in your constant protection. Forgive me for doubting you and trying to solve my own problems in my own ways.. Help me to confidently live out my faith so that others are drawn to Christ. In Jesus' name, Amen

Personal Reflection

Meditate on the reality of angelic protectors in your life. How does being mindful of the powerful warriors by your side impact your life and faith? Prayerfully ask God to show you at least one step you can take to walk more confidently, share your faith more boldly, or serve God more obediently.

_____

_____

_____

_____

_____

_____

_____

Day 20

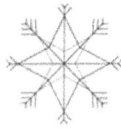

Day 21
Mary, Did You Know?

Today, I would like to look at a few verses from the birth narrative of Jesus. As we've already discussed, Mary did, in fact, know that her baby boy was God's promised Savior. As she rejoices that God has chosen her to be the mother of the Messiah, she humbly sings praise to the Father.

> *Oh, how my soul praises the Lord.*
> *How my spirit rejoices in God my Savior!*
> *For he took notice of his lowly servant girl,*
> *and from now on all generations will call me blessed.*
> *For the Mighty One is holy,*
> *and he has done great things for me.*
> *He shows mercy from generation to generation*
> *to all who fear him.*
> *His mighty arm has done tremendous things!*
> *He has scattered the proud and haughty ones.*
> *He has brought down princes from their thrones*
> *and exalted the humble.*
> ### *Luke 1:46–52*

Mary, the mother of Jesus, wasn't from a rich or powerful family. She hadn't done anything that the world would consider exceptional. Nonetheless, she was precious to God.

As I think about Mary, I'm reminded of a particular Christmas decoration from my childhood. When I was a little girl, my Gram had a battery powered Christmas bell. It was red and plastic, with fake holly hanging off of the bottom. When switched on, the bell would light up and play various Christmas melodies. The sound was horrible and the bell wasn't especially pretty, but I loved it anyway.

Every single Christmas, the bell hung in Gram's living room. As I got older, the bell became a little more worn each year and the sound became more garbled. Eventually, the only sound the bell could produce was an awful buzzing noise. Nonetheless, I treasured that bell even more and continued to display it even after my Gram was gone. Eventually the bell fell apart, but I still think about it every Christmas.

I cannot convey how much I loved that little bell. If you were to see it, you would be totally unimpressed. Compared to some of the breathtaking decorations on display during the holidays, the bell would seem quite ugly.

I believe that the way I feel about that bell is similar to the way God feels about me. I have many cracks and flaws. Sometimes I'm ugly, inside and out. I don't have anything to offer God that he couldn't do better without me. But, thankfully, God didn't choose me based on how I look or what I can do for him.

God wants a relationship with you simply because you bring him joy. Mary was an unimportant young girl according to worldly standards. She didn't have money, power, prestige, or any exceptional skills, but God was delighted to bless her and work through her.

Maybe you feel like you don't have anything to offer God today. You need to know that you bring joy to God's heart simply because you are *you*. God loves you as a Father, imperfections and all. Instead of fixating on your own imperfections today, fix your eyes on God's love.

Jesus, thank you for humbling yourself by being born as a child, living among us, and dying for my sins. Thank you for making me worthy of the Father's love. Help me remember that the most important things in life are not power and prestige, but love for God and people. Thank you for modeling selfless love and accepting me despite my flaws. Teach me to live with an attitude of humility and thanksgiving. Help me show the world your love through my life, my actions, and my words. In Jesus name, Amen

Personal Reflection

Read Luke 1–2 in entirety. As you read, take special notice of the mistakes and weaknesses of each individual. At the same time, pay attention to how God blesses them and works through them despite their flaws.

Scan the QR code for passages of Scripture

_____

_____

_____

_____

_____

_____

Day 21

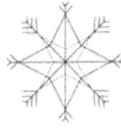

Day 22

O' Christmas Tree

A couple of weeks ago, I mentioned that my husband, Wesley, insists on having a live tree each year. Wesley has always been mesmerized by Christmas trees. As a small child, he would rise before everyone in the house on Christmas morning so that he could quietly bask in the glow of the tree and gaze at its beauty. I must agree that sitting by the Christmas tree is an experience that warms the heart.

Despite association with our Christian holiday, the Christmas tree actually originated in pagan culture. The trees and their boughs were used for both protective and celebratory purposes. People groups throughout the world believed that evergreens would repel evil spirits, ghosts, witches, and sickness.

In ancient Egypt, families brought evergreen branches into their homes during the winter solstice. They believed that the cooler temperatures and shorter days of winter occurred because their sun God, Ra, had grown ill. After the solstice, the shortest day of the year, Ra began to recover. The evergreens symbolized his triumph over death.

In northern Europe, the Vikings and Druids likewise associated evergreens with the eternal life of the gods. Temples and homes were decorated with the revered plants for worship and celebration. Some Nordic tribes brought entire trees into their homes, believing that tree spirits would bless the inhabitants and ward against evil.

Romans similarly celebrated the winter solstice by honoring their god of agriculture, Saturn. The feast of Saturnalia could last up to an entire week, during which raucous festivities and gift giving took place. As in ancient Egypt, homes were decorated with evergreen boughs to celebrate the gods' eternal life. Preferring not to cut down entire trees, living trees would be decorated outdoors where they grew. Later, when the Roman Empire converted to Christianity in the fourth century C.E., many of the Saturnalia traditions were absorbed into Christmas.

Although the Christmas tree has pagan origins, certain elements echo Scriptural truths. Trees have great significance throughout Scripture as locations where humans encounter God. God's presence by default creates a space defined by life and holiness. Although the biblical trees don't explicitly ward against evil, nothing nefarious can enter the sacred sphere.

The sacred space of the tree is often a place of testing in the lives of key biblical figures. In the Garden, Adam and Eve were presented with a choice between the Tree of Life and the Tree of knowledge— a choice between faith in God and life on their own terms. The burning bush, biologically and typologically similar to a tree, was the site of Moses' choice whether or not to accept God's calling. The cross upon which Jesus died, often called a "tree" by the authors of Scripture, tested the Savior's resolve to obey his Father and die on behalf of his people.

A tree even features prominently in the final chapter of Scripture. Although it isn't evergreen, the Tree of Life signifies eternal life for all who follow Christ. In Revelation 22, the tree sits in the center of a renewed Eden.

> *Then the angel showed me a river with the water of life, clear as crystal, flowing from the throne of God and of the Lamb. t flowed down the center of the main street. On each side of the river grew a tree of*

life, bearing twelve crops of fruit, with a fresh crop each month. The leaves were used for medicine to heal the nations. No longer will there be a curse upon anything. For the throne of God and of the Lamb will be there, and his servants will worship him.

Revelation 22:1–3

In the New Heaven and Earth, the Tree of Life is no longer a place of testing. Our Savior took every poor decision, every sin, every sickness, and every curse upon his own tree, the Cross. Never again can humanity be separated from God's love.

Christ is the embodiment of the Tree of Life. Through his work on the cross, we have direct access to the eternal life and power of God. As we celebrate the birth of our Savior, we can express gratitude for his victory over death. Like sitting in the glow of the Christmas tree, let's bask in the eternal glory of our Savior.

Lord, thank you for taking my sin to the Cross. Thank you for making a way for me to have an eternal, unbreakable relationship with my Father. Even though my sins and bad decisions can no longer separate me from your love, help me to honor your sacrifice by living righteously. As I live out my faith, help me to draw upon your power rather than operating in my own strength. I look forward to the day when I will dwell with you in the New Heaven and Earth forever. In Jesus' name, Amen

Personal Reflection

Take some time simply to bask in the presence of Jesus today. Find a quiet, distraction-free spot to pray, listen to worship music, listen for his voice, and worship his name.

Day 22

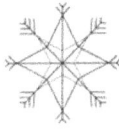

Day 23
Tree of Life

Yesterday, we talked about trees, a significant source of symbolism throughout the Bible. Trees are the most frequently mentioned living entity in the Bible, other than God and humans. From the opening chapters of Genesis to the closing chapters of Revelation, trees are a significant part of the biblical storyline.

Adam and Eve were presented with a variety of trees from which they could eat, and only one from which they couldn't. When Adam and Eve chose to eat from the Tree of Knowledge, they chose a life on their own terms rather than a life submitted to God. In doing so, they forfeited their right to the Tree of Life—the eternal life and power of God.

God gave humanity another chance to experience his life and power through Christ. Jesus is likened to a seed, sprout, and branching vine. He is the "seed" promised to Abraham (Gen 22:18) and the "tender shoot" prophesied by Isaiah (Isaiah 53:2). Jesus refers to himself as the "true vine" who gives life to believers (John 15:1–8).

Jesus is the embodiment of the Tree of Life, although Scripture doesn't specifically refer to Christ as such. He makes God's power available and invites people to choose life by "eating" what he offers. In John 6:57 Jesus explains, **"I live because of the living Father who sent me; in the same way, anyone who feeds on me will live because of me."**

Unfortunately, Jesus' offer was largely rejected during his lifetime, especially by his own people. He admonishes the Jewish leaders, "You search the Scriptures because you think they give you eternal life. But the Scriptures point to me! Yet you refuse to come to me to receive this life," (John 5:39–40). Not only did the religious leaders refuse to accept Jesus, they tried to destroy him by nailing him to a tree of death, the cross. Although many translations obscure the significance of the tree imagery by translating *zulon* as "cross," biblical authors repeatedly state that Christ died on a "tree." According to Acts 5:30, "The God of our Fathers raised Jesus up, whom you murdered by hanging him up on a tree," (my translation).

Of course, Jesus willingly went to the tree of death. Because he bore our sins with him to the cross, they were destroyed when he died. However, as the source of life and power, Jesus rose again. Because he conquered death and sin, he can offer the choice that Adam and Eve relinquished. We can once again choose to eat from the Tree of Life or continue living on our own terms.

If you are reading this book, I hope you've already chosen the Tree of Life. If not, I pray that you'll choose Jesus today. As you abide in him, you'll also become a metaphorical tree. Christ makes us fruitful branches (John 15:1–8), thriving trees (Psalm 1:3), flourishing palms, and cedars of Lebanon (Psalm 92:12). Next time you feel tired, weak, or insignificant, remember that you are a towering tree of righteousness. Through Christ, you have immeasurable power and life at your disposal. Draw upon him so that your roots grow deeper and your branches grow stronger.

Lord, thank you for dying on a tree and defeating death so that I can experience true life. Forgive me for treating your sacrifice lightly and living on my own terms instead of following you. Give me the diligence to grow my roots deep in you through prayer and Bible study. Help me walk confidently in your strength and bear good fruit. Equip me to nourish others as you nourish me. In Jesus' name, Amen

Personal Reflection

Imagine yourself as a tree and meditate on your health. Are you a towering oak or a scrawny sapling? Are your roots continually growing deeper? Is Christ the source of your nourishment and growth? Are your branches strong and fruitful? Ask God to show you one way you can grow healthier or stronger today.

_____

_____

_____

_____

_____

_____

_____

_____

_____

_____

_____

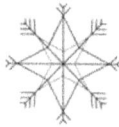

Day 24
Holly and Homicide

A little while back, we discussed holly, a beautiful evergreen plant with bright red berries. We also talked about the traditional symbolism in which the pointed leaves represent Jesus' crown of thorns and the berries represent his blood. According to the same tradition, holly exhibits one further trait of Christ. Because the hardy, evergreen plant thrives year-round, it has often been associated with the eternal life of our Savior.

It's easy to understand why holly would be associated with eternal life because it is nearly impossible to kill. The bushes can't be killed by overwatering, underwatering, or a hard freeze. The shrubs won't even die if you cut them down and pour weed killer over the stump. Sometimes it seems like holly bushes have eternal life!

Likewise, our Savior survived despite the Enemy's repeated schemes to have him killed. In Matthew 2:1–12, the murderous King Herod tried to deceive the Magi into revealing the location of the newborn Messiah. When that plan failed, Herod went into a fury and ordered that all boys under the age of two be slaughtered (Matthew 2:16). Jesus' family evaded Herod by fleeing to Egypt, then returned to Judea after Herod's death. Once Jesus grew to adulthood and began his public ministry, the religious leaders incessantly tried to find an excuse to have him executed.

When Satan finally succeeded in murdering the Messiah, his plan backfired. Although Jesus died on the cross, he rose again and defeated death. His sacrifice atoned for sin and effected restoration between God and humanity. Because of Jesus' redemptive work, you and I are freed from bondage and death. Paul explains that "God saved us and called us to live a holy life. He did this, not because we deserved it, but because that was his plan from before the beginning of time—to show us his grace through Christ Jesus. And now he has made all of this plain to us by the appearing of Christ Jesus, our Savior. He broke the power of death and illuminated the way to life and immortality through the Good News," (2 Timothy 1:9–10).

Because Jesus defeated death, his followers receive the gift of eternal life. Even better, we begin our eternal life the day we accept Christ. When we accept Jesus, we step into the first phase of eternity. As we follow him, Jesus empowers us to become agents of restoration and ministers of the Gospel. We work toward establishing his Kingdom on earth while we wait upon his Second Coming. Even if our current bodies die before he returns, we'll simply enter into the next phase of our eternal existence. We don't have to fear death as the end of our life. The passing of our current body is actually the beginning of eternity in God's presence. Let's embrace the new life we've received and live in the light of eternity.

Lord, thank you for being willing to die as a sacrifice for my sin. Thank you for making a way for me to have a relationship with my Heavenly Father. Thank you for defeating death so that I can spend eternity in your presence. Help me to live in the light of eternity and share the Gospel at every opportunity. Give me the wisdom to make choices that honor you and make a kingdom impact on my world. Empower me to do your will on this earth so that other people come to understand your goodness and mercy. I look forward to your return! In Jesus' name, Amen

Day 24

Personal Reflection

What does living in the light of eternity look like for you? How might it change the way you make decisions, interact with others, and utilize your resources? Would your priorities and goals change? Would you spend your time differently? Would you be more diligent about growing in faith and living for Christ? Prayerfully ask God to show you at least one step you can take to reorient your mindset and/or lifestyle in the light of eternity.

_____

_____

_____

_____

_____

_____

_____

_____

_____

_____

_____

_____

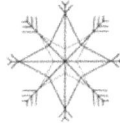

Day 25
What a Friend We Have in Jesus — Part 1

Yesterday, we talked about the death and resurrection of Christ, through which he earned eternal life for his followers. Yet, even before Jesus defeated death on the cross, he worked powerful miracles of healing and restoration. Our Savior is a compassionate friend who grieves when his people suffer and takes action on their behalf.

Lazarus, Mary, and Martha were dear friends of Jesus during his earthly life. Yet, when Jesus heard that Lazarus was ill, his response was puzzling. John records that "Although Jesus loved Martha, Mary, and Lazarus, he stayed where he was for the next two days," (John 11:5–6). If Jesus truly loved his friends and possessed the power to heal, why did he wait for two full days? Why didn't Jesus rush to the bedside of Lazarus? Why didn't he make haste to heal his friend?

By the time Jesus and his disciples arrived at the home of Lazarus, they discovered that the man had already been in his tomb for four days (John 11:17). That length of time was not random, nor was Jesus surprised that Lazarus was already dead. Let me explain.

In Jesus' time and culture, the dead were placed in carved out stone tombs rather than being buried or cremated. According to Jewish tradition, the soul hovered around the body for about three days in hopes of being reunited with the body. The belief was well founded since sometimes people actually did get up and leave the tomb! In the absence of modern medical technology, very ill or comatose patients were sometimes mistaken for dead. Thus, the family of the deceased could only be certain that their loved one was truly gone after about three days had passed and the body began to stink.

When Jesus arrived in Bethany, Lazarus was on day four of his entombment. Mary and Martha believed that their brother was truly and permanently gone, and their situation was dire. The women weren't only mourning the loss of a brother, but the loss of their security. As unmarried females, Mary and Martha would face extreme difficulty providing for themselves. I can't help but think that they must have felt confused, hurt, and even angry at Jesus.

Mary and Martha knew Jesus possessed the power to heal, but he hadn't healed their brother. Jesus was traveling across the countryside doing miracles for everyone else, yet it seemed as though he had failed his friends. John records, "When Mary arrived and saw Jesus, she fell at his feet and said, "Lord, if only you had been here, my brother would not have died,"" (John 11:32).

When enduring a difficult season of life, it sometimes feels as though Jesus has abandoned you. Maybe you prayed fervently and trusted him to move on your behalf, but he didn't rescue you from your trial. Perhaps you trusted him to deliver healing, promotion, or vindication, but he didn't provide the outcome for which you hoped. However, God may be doing something even greater than you imagine. Jesus might not move when or how you expect, but he will *never* fail you.

Jesus didn't move in the way that Mary, Martha, or Lazarus expected. Jesus let Lazarus die and stay in the grave for four days so that everyone knew, without a shadow of doubt, that the man was dead. John narrates the sequence of events as Jesus approached the tomb.

> *"Roll the stone aside," Jesus told them. But Martha, the dead man's sister, protested, "Lord, he has been dead for four days. The smell will be terrible." Jesus*

responded, "Didn't I tell you that you would see God's glory if you believe?" So they rolled the stone aside. Then Jesus looked up to heaven and said, "Father, thank you for hearing me. You always hear me, but I said it out loud for the sake of all these people standing here, so that they will believe you sent me." Then Jesus shouted, "Lazarus, come out!" And the dead man came out, his hands and feet bound in graveclothes, his face wrapped in a headcloth. Jesus told them, "Unwrap him and let him go!" Many of the people who were with Mary believed in Jesus when they saw this happen.
John 11:39–45

Jesus didn't rush to Bethany when he heard Lazarus was sick. Jesus did not cure his friend's sickness or prevent his death. Jesus certainly did not provide a miracle in the way that Mary, Martha, and Lazarus hoped. Jesus did, however, allow his friends to be a part of an even greater miracle than the one for which they had hoped and prayed. In fact, Mary, Martha, and Lazarus became participants in one of the greatest miracles of Scripture. Not only did Jesus heal Lazarus, but he raised him from the dead, and Jesus' display of love and power was so great that many who saw the miracle began to follow Jesus.

Are you hoping and praying Jesus will move on your behalf? Remember that he may not move when or how you expect, but he will *never* fail you. Let's surrender the expectations we place upon our God and the guidelines within which we expect him to work. Let's trust him unconditionally and allow him to do a greater miracle than we could imagine.

Lord, thank you for working in my life and moving on my behalf even when I don't see you at work or understand your plan. Help me to trust you without reservation even when you operate differently than I anticipate. Forgive me for my moments of doubt, and grow my faith so that I'm not shaken by the unexpected. Align my heart with yours so that I desire your will above my own. I pray that my faith in you would be an encouragement and inspiration to others. I pray that you would work through me in such a way that others would place their faith in you. In Jesus' name, Amen

Personal Reflection

What expectations or limitations are you placing on God? Meditate on any current life situations for which you are praying. Will you be disappointed if the Lord doesn't respond in a specific way or in a specific time? Write down 3–5 of your top prayer needs. Prayerfully commit each one to the Lord, then confess your trust in God's perfect plan. Thank God for his goodness and ask him to grow your faith.

_____

_____

_____

_____

_____

_____

_____

_____

Day 26
What a Friend We Have in Jesus — Part 2

Yesterday, we talked about the death of Lazarus and the response of Jesus. Our Messiah didn't heal his friend in the way that Lazarus, Mary, and Martha expected. Instead, he allowed them to be a part of an even greater miracle. As Jesus raised Lazarus from the dead, many people were moved to place their faith in the Lord.

Although Jesus was fully aware he had the power to resurrect Lazarus, he was nonetheless distressed by his friend's illness and death, as well as the grief of Mary and Martha. When Jesus arrived and saw Mary weeping, he was "deeply moved" (John 11:33). As he approached Lazarus' tomb, "Jesus wept" and was again "deeply moved" (John 11:35, 38). Our Savior was not cold and dispassionate about the death of his friend and the grief of the sisters.

In fact, the Greek word used to describe Jesus' emotional state in John 11 is *embrimaomai*, which indicates extreme distress. The term can denote anger, agitation, or concern so intense that it is accompanied by a physical expression such as weeping, moaning, or yelling. Along such lines, Jesus is so distressed by the suffering of his people that he takes action. Jesus cares about *your* need and will move on *your* behalf.

Jesus hurts when his people hurt. He is grieved by sickness and death. He is angered by oppression and injustice. He mourns for broken marriages and fractured relationships. He is distressed by every sin that harms his people and corrupts the perfect world he created.

Jesus will eventually return, wipe away sin, and punish sinners. However, he delays out of compassion. Peter explains, "The Lord isn't really being slow about his promise, as some people think. No, he is being patient for your sake. He does not want anyone to be destroyed, but wants everyone to repent," (2 Peter 3:9).

While we await the return of Christ and the end of suffering, we are called to emulate our Savior. When we encounter suffering, we should be so grieved that we aid the afflicted. When we see injustice, we should be moved to oppose the oppressor. Through the work of Christ on our behalf, we are empowered to follow in the footsteps of our Savior and take action!

Lord, thank you for your compassion toward me and for extending your grace and mercy to each person in the world. Help me to follow your example of sacrificial love for all people. Forgive me for my apathy toward those who are hurting in my community and my world. Make my heart tender toward all people. Equip and empower me to help the helpless and defend the powerless. Allow me to be a vehicle of your mercy and salvation. Show me how I can use my resources to reach both the oppressed and the oppressor with the Gospel message. In Jesus' name, Amen

Personal Reflection

As you go through your day, seek opportunities to show compassion to people who need love, encouragement, or grace. Also look for practical ways to help people who are hurting.

_____

_____

_____

_____

Day 26

Day 27
Wilderness Wandering

We don't know much about the early life of Jesus. The authors of Scripture are largely silent about the period between Jesus' birth and public ministry. Similarly, Luke provides little information on the years between the conception and adult ministry of John the Baptist. Luke simply states, "John grew up and became strong in spirit. And he lived in the wilderness until he began his public ministry to Israel," (Luke 1:80).

John spent a substantial period of time in the Judean wilderness. The region is primarily characterized by dry, desert conditions. Food and water are scarce. The days are hot and the nights are cold. The only shelter available consists of rocky caves.

The Judean desert provides ideal conditions for testing and strengthening the resilience of anyone brave enough to spend extended time in the harsh terrain. Indeed, throughout Scripture, the wilderness serves as a place of testing and preparation. Although little vegetation grows in the desert, faith flourishes. In the isolated and barren land, the Father teaches his children to follow him. As God's people trust him for provision and protection, they learn to abide in his presence.

We can only speculate why and for how long John lived in the Judean wilderness, but as the son of a priest, he likely knew the significance of seasons in the desert. In fact, his public ministry began in the wilderness. John's preaching was so powerful that people came from all over the region to hear him and be baptized. Matthew describes the early days of John's ministry.

> *In those days John the Baptist came to the Judean wilderness and began preaching. His message was, "Repent of your sins and turn to God, for the Kingdom of Heaven is near."* . . . *People from Jerusalem and from all of Judea and all over the Jordan Valley went out to see and hear John.*
>
> ### Matthew 3:1–2, 5

As John exhorted his hearers to repent and turn to God, he prepared the way for Jesus, who likewise spent time in the wilderness. For 40 days, the Son of God dwelled in the inhospitable terrain while being tested by Satan (Matthew 4:1–2).

I find it significant that God prepared most of the important figures in Scripture in isolation and obscurity. In addition to Jesus and John, Abraham, Moses, and David all spent extended time in the wilderness. More importantly, each man exhibited a heart of humility. Moses, in particular, is described as the humblest person on earth (Numbers 12:3). Of Jesus, Zechariah says, "Look, your king is coming to you. He is righteous and victorious, yet he is humble, riding on a donkey—riding on a donkey's colt," (Zechariah 9:9). One would expect a king to ride upon a powerful steed, but our Lord chose to ride a diminutive donkey.

If the King of Kings was willing to live humbly, we should be privileged to follow his example. Jesus did not seek fame, demand worship, or accumulate wealth. Before his brief, three-year ministry, the Son of God remained in obscurity for 30 years while preparing for his purpose. We should likewise embrace our seasons of unseen preparation. Next time you feel unseen, underappreciated, or over-looked, think about Jesus and thank him for humbly leading the way.[1]

Lord, thank you for modeling humility and teaching me to have a heart that honors God. I repent of taking offense when I don't receive recognition or acclaim. Forgive me for becoming angry with you when I don't receive the promotions and blessings I think I've earned. I acknowledge that everything I have is from you. I thank you that I have value in your eyes, even when the world doesn't acknowledge my worth. Help me grow in humility so that I can serve you more effectively. In Jesus' name, Amen

Personal Reflection

Prayerfully ask God how you can grow in humility so that you can serve more effectively. If you are in a wilderness season, do you need to embrace your obscurity and lean into God's process of preparation? If you are in a season of prominence, do you need to sacrifice your own accolades in order to honor those around you? If you are in a season of abundance, do you need to grow in gratitude and surrender your resources to a greater degree?

_____

_____

_____

_____

---

[1] For further study on thriving in the hidden seasons of life, I recommend *Anonymous* by Dr. Alicia Britt Chole (Thomas Nelson, 2011).

Day 27

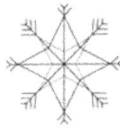

Day 28
Apocalypse Now

When the covid pandemic hit in 2020, many believers began to wonder if the apocalypse was imminent. As the year progressed, the state of our country went from bad to worse with sudden financial recession, bitter racial tensions, and rampant west coast fires. In the years following the pandemic, the U.S. faced radical inflation, a divisive presidential election, and the invasion of Ukraine by Russia, which many feared would provoke a third world war. Those who were concerned about an impending apocalypse became even more certain that it was near.

You may be surprised to hear that I believe we are actually in the middle of an apocalypse, just not in the way you might think. In biblical Greek, "apocalypse" simply means "revelation." So, an apocalypse is a moment when God reveals his perspective. Typically, an apocalypse signifies the end of one thing and the beginning of something new. It is a moment when new and exciting possibilities become available.

Over the last few years, God has certainly opened up fresh opportunities. Although the pandemic created problems, it also offered a respite from the frenetic pace at which we live. It afforded families more time together. It spurred many people to reflect upon their faith and draw nearer to God.

Our lives may never be exactly the same as they were before the pandemic, but God is revealing new possibilities. Instead of mourning

Day 28

the past, we can eagerly anticipate the future. Every ending is simply an avenue for God to deliver fresh blessings. The prophet Isaiah exhorts, "But forget [the past]—it is nothing compared to what I am going to do. For I am about to do something new. See, I have already begun! Do you not see it? I will make a pathway through the wilderness. I will create rivers in the dry wasteland," (Isaiah 43:18–9). You may feel like you are in the middle of a desert wasteland, but as we discussed yesterday, God is strengthening and preparing you for the next season. Your Father wants to do something new and exciting in your life!

Now in regard to *the* final apocalypse, Scripture repeatedly tells us that we simply won't know when to expect it (Mark 13:33–35; Matthew 24). So, in the meantime, let's make the most of every opportunity. What new thing is God doing in your life today?

Lord, I eagerly anticipate the opportunity to worship in your presence when you return. Until that time, help me remain alert for new opportunities that you place before me. Show me how I can be part of building your kingdom on this earth. Give me the perseverance to serve you diligently so that when I meet you, I will hear you say, "well done." Thank you for allowing me to be part of what you are doing on this earth. In Jesus' name, Amen

Personal Reflection

Meditate on the opportunities that God may be opening up in the new year. Consider how you might grow in faith, serve God, and love others in new ways. Write down your thoughts below and pray over the possibilities.

Day 29
A Rat's Nest — Part 1

Apparently, rodents don't like being cold any more than people do. I learned just how much rodents like to stay warm a couple of winters ago. My first indication was rat poop in the garden shed, but since it was cold outside, I deferred the problem to spring. I figured that once the weather was warm again, the dogs would chase the rodents away and I would clean the shed. My plan didn't work out as I hoped, as the rodents soon made their way to our house.

A few weeks prior to Christmas, I had hidden stocking candy in the attic. The sweet snacks served as an inviting stockpile for my rodent friends. The mice and rats loved the special treats! Fortunately, I discovered the half-eaten candies early enough to purchase new stocking stuffers.

The next incident was even more problematic. One morning, as my husband was pulling out of the driveway in his car, he discovered that his brakes didn't work. After employing the emergency brake to stop the car, then having it towed to the repair shop, we learned that rats had chewed through several cables. The mechanic informed us that rodents love shacking up in car engines because the environment is comfy and warm.

Vehicular vandalism was the final straw. By then, however, the rodent problem was too pervasive to handle on our own. We called pest control and began the process of deep cleaning. Regretfully, we probably could have avoided the car repair bill and the pest control bill if I had simply addressed the problem as soon as it began.

When we procrastinate, problems fester and grow. They may even spawn more problems that spread out and consume valuable resources, both literally and figuratively. The author of Proverbs describes what happens when we neglect problems. He says, "I walked by the field of a lazy person, the vineyard of one with no common sense. I saw that it was overgrown with nettles. It was covered with weeds, and its walls were broken down," (Proverbs 24:30–31). Whether we neglect problems due to laziness, apathy, or folly, they will multiply like rodents and cause a nasty mess.

Even after our rats were gone, their droppings and nests cluttered our property. Similarly, our problems aren't easily eliminated, nor do they remain confined to one area. They draw resources from everywhere and spread their mess to all areas of our lives. Problems drain us physically, emotionally, relationally, and mentally. Even when problems are finally resolved, they often require clean up and damage control.

I hope you learn from my mistakes. Don't let any rodents shack up in your house, your garden shed, your car, or your life!

Lord, thank you for giving me the abilities and resources I need to handle my problems wisely. Help me to deal with each one immediately so that they don't have time to fester, grow, or multiply. Help me guard against procrastination, laziness, and fear over confronting challenges. Thank you in advance for providing me with strength and discernment. When I am frustrated or upset, help me to seek resolution instead of burying my thoughts and feelings beneath distractions. Give me the clarity to find the root causes of obstacles so that I can turn them into opportunities for growth. In Jesus' name, Amen

Personal Reflection

Are there any problems, obstacles, or difficulties you have been avoiding? Make a list of any issues that are causing you worry or mental turmoil. Pray over each and ask God to help you discern which issues require action and which are beyond your control. Prayerfully release the things that you can't control to your Father. For the rest, ask God to show you how you can take one step toward resolution.

_____

_____

_____

_____

_____

_____

_____

_____

_____

_____

_____

_____

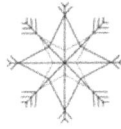

Day 30
A Rat's Nest — Part 2

Yesterday, we talked about the rodent problem my family had a few years ago. Rats and their nests must be dealt with before they get out of control. Even after I got rid of my literal rodents, their nests remained in the garden shed and attic. Rats' nests are messy piles constructed of shredded fabric, dead leaves, and any other debris the rodents can find. They will use virtually anything to construct their nest. Their only requirement is a nearby source of food and water.

Even if we don't have any massive looming problems, our lives can still be a chaotic mess. We frantically go from task to task, get through each day by the skin of our teeth, and shred our mental and physical health in the process. We hope that the frenetic pace won't last forever and that it will eventually yield fulfillment. Constant busyness, however, is not a biblical tenant. Paul offers sage advice on living effectively for Jesus. He instructs, "So be careful how you live. Don't live like fools, but like those who are wise. Make the most of every opportunity in these evil days. Don't act thoughtlessly, but understand what the Lord wants you to do," (Ephesians 5:15–17).

Instead of cramming everything possible into our days and weeks, Paul advises us to be intentional and thoughtful about how we use our time and resources. Sometimes, saying "no" is just as important as saying "yes." Instead of allowing your life to become a rats' nest of random obligations, ask for God's help aligning your time and resources with your calling.

Lord, thank you for giving my life purpose and meaning. Help me manage my time and resources well in order to accomplish your will for my life. Give me the wisdom to create healthy patterns of work, service, and rest. Help me be thoughtful about when to say "yes" and when to say "no." Show me any areas of my life that are creating clutter, stress, or distraction. Help me to minimize distractions and maximize opportunities so that I can serve you faithfully. In Jesus' name, Amen

Personal Reflection

Take time to pray over your calendar and your obligations. Ask God to show you any areas of life that are detracting from his purpose for you. If you are overly busy, ask God to show you what needs to be removed from your life. If you have an abundance of free time, ask God to open up doors of opportunity to serve him.

_____

_____

_____

_____

_____

_____

_____

_____

_____

_____

Day 31
Rats and Religion

The last couple of days, we've been talking about the rodent problem my family dealt with a few years ago. While working to get rid of the rodents and clean up their mess, I discovered that several factors had contributed to the infestation. The foremost issue is that our home sits a short distance from the banks of a pond, which is desirable real estate for rodents during the spring and summer. When temperatures drop in the winter, our home becomes an ideal place to shelter from the cold.

As the weather cools, I also move a large number of outdoor plants to the garden shed and garage. When the temperature is above freezing, I like to keep the doors open so the plants get sunlight. Unfortunately, I learned that my open doors signify an open invitation to any rodents seeking warmth and shelter.

To prevent further incursions, I had to take proactive steps. First, I signed a monthly contract with a pest control service. Then, upon the recommendation of my technician, I employed several further strategies. I ensured that all external doors remained closed. I plugged holes where the rats had chewed through the shed floor to create additional entrances. I also soaked old towels in peppermint oil and stuffed the scented fabric into every crack and cranny I could find in the garage, attic, and shed. (Apparently, rodents don't like peppermint.)

Our home still has the occasional visitor, but because we are watchful and diligent, the rodents don't stick around. Likewise, Paul teaches us to deal with deception decisively. He warns the Corinthian church:

> *But I fear that somehow your pure and undivided devotion to Christ will be corrupted, just as Eve was deceived by the cunning ways of the serpent. You happily put up with whatever anyone tells you, even if they preach a different Jesus than the one we preach, or a different kind of Spirit than the one you received, or a different kind of gospel than the one you believed.*
> **2 Corinthians 11:3–4**

Corinth was a city full of deception and debauchery. As in our culture today, many people considered themselves spiritual. Unfortunately, their spirituality was a self-indulgent imitation of true faith. Their false religion was full of greed, sensuality, and lies.

Members of the Corinthian church struggled to maintain their identity in Christ without succumbing to the temptations of their culture. Some church leaders even taught that faith in Christ was compatible with prevailing cultural and religious norms. Paul chastised the church for putting up with such deception.

Tolerating false teaching in our lives, families, or churches is like letting rodents move in. We may not initially be concerned over a few little mice. We may feel confident that we can get rid of the rodents at a more convenient time. But before we realize it, they've had babies, invited their relatives over, and eaten our Christmas candy.

As in ancient Rome, our culture offers many enticing avenues for compromising our faith. We must be proactive to remain rooted in God's truth and live according to his teaching.

Lord, thank you for the truth of Scripture that makes the Gospel clear. Help me to be proactive and diligent in my Bible study so that I'll be able to discern truth from lies. Give me the wisdom to take proactive steps to guard against deception in my life, my family, and my church. Empower me to speak the truth in love to anyone who shares a false gospel or fake spirituality. Provide opportunities for me to share my faith and help me speak unashamedly. Go before me to open the eyes of those who are blinded by deception. In Jesus' name, Amen

Personal Reflection

Throughout your day, be on guard against the deception of the enemy or the temptation to compromise. Be inwardly proactive as you remain diligent to think, speak, and behave in ways that are true to your faith. Also be outwardly proactive and seek opportunities to lovingly share the truth of the Gospel.

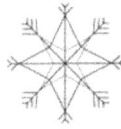

Day 32

Joy to the World (and More Lessons from Rodents)

Today, I would like to talk about joy. Joy may feel like an elusive emotion, but it is actually an essential facet of our relationship with God. Cultivating a mindset of joy empowers us to walk in God's strength and persevere in our faith.

Once again, the rodents who moved into my house provide a helpful illustration. Let me briefly pause, however, to apologize for writing so many devotionals about rats, especially during the Christmas season. I promise that today will be the final rodent devo. To make it more fun, why don't we picture the rats and mice in little Santa hats as they thrived in my attic and devoured our Christmas candy.

Because the well-fed, festive little rodents rapidly proliferated beyond my control, I had to take decisive action. I've already mentioned several proactive strategies I implemented, which included hiring a pest control service. The pest control technician immediately implemented his own strategy: poison traps.

I was concerned that my dogs might ingest poison, so I asked the technician to explain exactly how the traps worked. The design is brilliant in its simplicity. The trap is simply a small black box with a delicious snack inside. The snack will kill rodents, but it can't be classified strictly as a poison. The substance is a diuretic, which causes excess urination and severe dehydration. Upon ingestion, the rodents become insatiably thirsty and leave their homes to seek water. Eventually, they die of dehydration, but only after they have departed from your yard, garage, or house. If my dogs somehow managed to get the "tasty snack" out of the box, they would simply be thirsty for a couple of days and experience no lasting discomfort.

The desirable, tasty rat poison reminds me of Proverbs 6:32. The proverb reads, "A man who commits adultery has no sense; whoever does so destroys himself." Although the verse specifies adultery, I believe that it can apply to any activity that is desirable but ultimately destructive.

As humans, our sin nature sometimes causes us to thirst for harmful substances or damaging pursuits. While our indulgence might bring momentary happiness, the pleasure will ultimately lead to pain. Furthermore, since the enjoyment is fleeting, we continue to thirst for more. Because the thirst can never be quenched, the temporary pleasure ends up siphoning our joy rather than fulfilling our soul.

Lasting joy can only be found in God's presence (Psalm 16:11). The fullness of joy that comes from our Father is the only pursuit that can quench our souls. In fact, the love of God enables us to overcome unhealthy desires so that we can abide in his joy.

Unlike rats and dogs, God has given us the faculty to make wise choices. As God's children, we have the capacity to forego momentary temptation for the sake of lasting rewards. As we resist temptation, we follow the example of our Savior who denied the needs of his flesh as he died on the cross. Jesus held the power to alleviate his own suffering, but instead endured pain "because of the joy awaiting him," (Hebrews 2:2; see also Matthew 4:1–11). Jesus gave up temporary relief in order to win a better prize—reconciliation between God and his people. The birth, life, death, and resurrection of Jesus is literally the greatest cause for joy in the history of the world! Let's be intentional about sharing the source of our joy as we celebrate our Savior throughout the Christmas season.

Lord, thank you for modeling a life of love, obedience, and joy. Thank you for denying your own needs and sacrificing your own life so that I can have access to the Father, the source of all joy. Help me follow your example as I seek to walk in obedience and forgo temporary pleasures. I repent of indulging in disobedient patterns that dishonor your sacrifice. Reveal any self-destructive tendencies in my life and help me resist harmful temptations. Teach me to walk in joy as I grow closer to you and experience a greater measure of your presence. Give me opportunities to share the reason for my joy. In Jesus' Name, Amen

Personal Reflection

Read Psalm 16 in entirety and list every blessing that God showers upon those who follow his guidance. Thank him for each one!

Scan the QR code for passages of Scripture

_____

_____

_____

_____

_____

Day 32

Day 33
Mirror, Mirror — Part 1

Over the holidays, we tend to be less physically active while simultaneously indulging in more rich foods and sweet desserts. Typically, our pants get tighter while our scales go higher. Once January 1st rolls around, crowds flock to gyms and multitudes begin fad diets.

Body image is a struggle for many people, non-Christian and Christian alike. At times, we base our self-worth more on our weight than our identity in Christ. When we fixate on weight, our emotional, mental, and spiritual well-being become tied to our appearance rather than being rooted in God's love.

Prioritizing outward appearance over inner wellness is antithetical to God's perspective. According to 1 Samuel 16:7, "The Lord doesn't see things the way you see them. People judge by outward appearance, but the Lord looks at the heart." God sees who we truly are, and he loves us regardless of clothing size or body weight. Additionally, our Father desires that we foster health in our spirit, mind, and body. As people who seek to reflect the character of God, we should strive to align our perspective with that of our Lord.

If we root our self-worth in anything other than the love of our Father, our entire perspective on life becomes skewed. When we believe our own self-assessment more than God's truth, we become our own idol. We begin to create strategies, often unhealthy ones, to become more attractive, thin, muscular, or whatever physical traits we prize. Sadly, fixating on outward appearance makes spiritual growth and emotional health nearly impossible.

An obsession with physical appearance can be just as damaging as an addiction to drugs or alcohol. Just as with any addiction, if you struggle with body image, God isn't angry—he wants to free you from bondage!

So, how can you develop a healthy perspective, take care of your physical body, and refuse to fixate on weight or appearance? First, I recommend ditching the scale, which often functions like a drug pusher. When you see you've dropped a pound, you receive a hit of feel-good hormones, and you're happy about yourself all day long. If the number goes up, however, you feel worthless, and you may even take extreme measures to get that number back down. Weighing isn't inherently sinful, but linking your emotional well-being with your weight is self-destructive.

Second, when you look in the mirror, express gratitude. Instead of berating yourself for traits you dislike, thank God for your physical body. Even if you feel unattractive, you can give thanks for parts of your body that are strong. You can give thanks for a body that gets you from place to place. You can give thanks for eyes that see and ears that hear. If you're a parent, you can thank God for your body's ability to create life!

Third, seek a partner in your journey toward becoming healthier. Ask a friend or spiritual mentor to provide regular accountability and encouragement. Begin praying about who you might ask, and we'll spend another day on this subject tomorrow.

Heavenly Father, thank you for creating my body and giving me the ability to serve you. Thank you for hands that are capable of helping others. Thank you for feet that take me where you want me to go. Thank you for five senses that enable me to enjoy the good world you've created. Give me the maturity to focus on the blessings of my physical body rather than aspects of my appearance with which I am dissatisfied. Help me to root my identity so firmly in you that I wouldn't be discouraged by the number on a scale or the size of my clothing. Show me someone in my life with whom I can partner in my journey of becoming healthy and whole. In Jesus' name, Amen.

Personal Reflection

Each time you look in the mirror today, thank God for one aspect of your physical body.

_____

_____

_____

_____

_____

_____

_____

_____

_____

_____

_____

_____

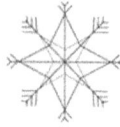

Day 34
Mirror, Mirror — Part 2

Have you ever looked in the mirror and lamented over your weight? Have you ever asked someone, "Does this outfit make me look fat"? In our culture, we tend to have an excessively negative attitude toward fat. We often view body fat as a personal flaw that renders us somehow less worthy of love.

To the contrary, fat is an essential element in the bodies of both humans and animals. Elephant seals, which can grow to over 8,000 pounds, depend upon their excess fat. The thick blubber keeps them warm in frigid waters. It also creates a natural buoyancy that helps the seals swim efficiently with little energy expenditure.

During mating season, the seals live on land for up to four months. Since their diet consists of undersea creatures, they go without food for their entire stay on the beach. As they fast, their ample blubber is metabolized for both water and nutrition. By the end of mating season, elephant seals can use up to 40% of their body fat.

Bears that hibernate, such as brown bears and grizzlies, need fat stores for survival. During the summer and fall, some of them eat nearly 100 pounds of food a day to prepare for winter. While they slumber through the cold months, excess fat is metabolized for energy to stay alive. For female bears, who give birth during the winter, fat stores are even more vital. Since they don't leave the den, excess fat stores are used to keep the mother healthy as well as produce milk for nursing cubs.

In humans, body fat plays a variety of essential roles. Fat surrounds and cushions vital organs. It serves as a concentrated energy source for the body and brain, as opposed to carbohydrates and protein, which produce less than half the energy of fat. Fat is the only vehicle through which the vitamins A, D, E, and K can be absorbed. Surprisingly, fat tissue even sends and receives messages throughout the body, keeping the immune system and neural pathways operating properly.

Certainly, excessive body fat is unhealthy and overindulgence in fatty foods can create health problems. However, anything in excess becomes harmful. We must shift our mindset away from seeing fat as our enemy. Body fat is not inherently bad. In fact, an excessively low body fat percentage can cause health problems just as severe as one that is too high.

Yesterday, we talked about three strategies for developing a healthier attitude toward our physical bodies. First, I recommended ditching the scale. Our self-worth should not be determined by our weight. Second, we must learn to appreciate our bodies and express gratitude for their benefits. Third, finding an accountability partner can foster healthier habits and lasting change.

Today, I would like to offer two further strategies. Your fourth strategy is to stop thinking of foods as good or bad. Instead, remember that food is your fuel. Foster a mindset in which you choose foods that benefit your body and help it function optimally. As you learn to love your body, you'll want to treat it well and take good care of it.

Fifth, agree with what God says about you in his Word. Make a list of scriptures that encourage you. Speak them over yourself and write them on your mirror. You may even want to set reminders on your phone with verses or phrases from God's Word.

Your body is a wonderful creation with so much greater worth than is reflected by the number on a scale of the percentage of your body fat. Let's echo the words of the Psalmist to God, "You made all the delicate, inner parts of my body and knit me together in my mother's womb. Thank you for making me so wonderfully complex! Your workmanship is marvelous—how well I know it" (Psalm 139:13–14).

Heavenly Father, thank you for giving me a body that is intricately fashioned and wonderfully complex. Forgive me for failing to appreciate the beauty of my body. Forgive me for focusing more on my appearance than my health. Help me to make wise choices in regard to nutrition and exercise. Equip me to steward well the body you've given me. Show me a person in my life with whom I can partner in my journey of becoming healthy and whole. Teach me to live in health and wholeness so that I can help other people in my life grow healthier. In Jesus' name, Amen

Personal Reflection

* Continue fostering gratitude today. Each time you look in the mirror, thank God for one aspect of your physical body.
* Continue to pray about asking a friend or spiritual mentor to provide regular accountability and encouragement. If God places someone on your heart, reach out to them today.

Begin making a list of Scriptures that inspire you to take care of your body and root your self-worth in God's Word. Here are a few to get you started: Romans 12:1–2; 1 Corinthians 6:19–20; 9: 24–27.

If any others come to mind, write them below.

_____

_____

Day 35
Bird of Paradise

When I began my yearly fast in January 2022, I was in an extraordinarily busy season of life. By the end of the first day, I had eaten very little, but I'd also spent very little time with God. As I finally sat down to pray, God immediately spoke to my heart and said, "You are like that bird." Of course, that doesn't mean anything to you so let me explain.

I love watching nature documentaries because they allow me to view remote parts of creation and bizarre creatures that I will probably never see in person. I especially love watching unusual birds and their behaviors.

While watching BBC Earth, I learned that roughly fifty bird of paradise species exist. One type, in particular, is more exuberant and enterprising than the average. The male six-plumed bird of paradise is fastidious about his habitat. He scurries about on the forest floor removing sticks, leaves, and debris from his space. He even scrubs surrounding branches to a smooth finish. Once the area is clean and tidy, he calls out to attract nearby females and begins dancing. The proud male puffs out his plumage, then twirls, dips, and hops in hopes of winning a mate. The whole frenzied process is truly entertaining to watch.

When God told me I was "like that bird," I knew he was referring to my frenetic activity. Although my work was done in his service, I was failing to find a balance between serving and sitting at his feet.

A few days ago, we talked about Lazarus, Mary, and Martha. I've always felt a kinship with Martha, who hosted Jesus and served him with vigor. Opening her home was a risky and sacrificial gesture, as Jesus was viewed as a seditious figure by the authorities. Yet Martha, the epitome of hospitality, welcomed Jesus and prepared a meal for his followers.

As Martha bustled around serving guests, her sister Mary sat at the feet of Jesus. I can relate to Martha's frustration when she asked Jesus, "Lord, doesn't it seem unfair to you that my sister just sits here while I do all the work? Tell her to come and help me" (Luke 10:40).

While Martha's desire to serve Jesus wasn't wrong, her priorities were misaligned. Martha had direct access to the Messiah, yet she was concerned with mealtime chores. In his kindness, Jesus gently helped his host reevaluate her priorities: "But the Lord said to her, "My dear Martha, you are worried and upset over all these details! There is only one thing worth being concerned about. Mary has discovered it, and it will not be taken away from her,"" (Luke 10:41–42).

You and I have direct access to our Lord through the presence of the Holy Spirit. But we often spend so much time doing things *for* him that we neglect to spend time *with* him. Serving Jesus is important, but sitting at his feet is vital.

Lord, thank you for providing direct access to your presence through the Holy Spirit. Help me to find a healthy balance between serving you and sitting at your feet. Give me the discernment to rightly prioritize my time and the discipline to keep my priorities in order. In Jesus Name, Amen.

Personal Reflection

Revisit the personal reflection and your notes from Day 3. First, consider whether you've maintained the time management boundaries you set. Have you better aligned your priorities and your schedule? Consider whether you need to reassess or reaffirm the adjustments you decided to make. Second, evaluate your routine even more acutely than before. Write down any tasks and activities that are unproductive, inefficient, or simply less important than time with God. Finally, ask God to help you adjust your schedule in such a way that he is your first priority.

_____

_____

_____

_____

_____

_____

_____

_____

_____

_____

_____

_____

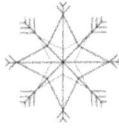

Day 36
Frogs, Snails, and Puppy-dog Tails

During the fall and winter, I transfer a multitude of outdoor plants into the house so that they don't freeze in the cold. I bring plants into my bedroom, bathroom, dining room, office, and kitchen. When I run out of reasonable surfaces, I begin covering the kitchen table in potted foliage. Although I have to move the plants temporarily for meals, I consider the task a minor inconvenience. Rather, I used to consider the task a minor inconvenience until the plants caused a major issue at dinner one evening.

While we were eating a hearty meal of breakfast-for-dinner, I happened to glance at Asher's plate. I was so stunned by what I saw that I couldn't process the visual information. Once I determined that my eyes weren't playing tricks, I instructed Asher to stop eating. I knew he hadn't seen what I'd seen or he would have reacted with emphatic disgust. You see, halfway across Asher's plate, gliding up a mound of scrambled eggs, was a snail.

As expected, Asher was repulsed by his dinner guest. My genteel older son is not fond of slugs, snails, or bugs. Had the snail oozed onto Abel's plate, my younger son would've been delighted to make a new friend and share his dinner. For Asher, on the other hand, seeing a snail crawl across his plate decisively killed any remaining appetite. Although we had plenty more food, he was DONE.

I humbly apologized and acknowledged that the snail almost certainly came from one of my plants. Although no one was angry with me, they kindly requested that plants no longer be stored on the kitchen table. I was happy to comply since I have no desire to entertain snails or slugs for dinner myself.

Like the snail on the dinner plate, our actions sometimes have unintended consequences. Life is full of unexpected moments, unplanned incidents, and unwelcome surprises. Fortunately, the more we cultivate godly wisdom and approach decisions thoughtfully, the better we can prepare for whatever the future may hold. Paul exhorts, "So be careful how you live. Don't live like fools, but like those who are wise. Make the most of every opportunity in these evil days. Don't act thoughtlessly, but understand what the Lord wants you to do," (Ephesians 5:15–17). When I stockpiled greenery on the table, I made a thoughtless choice. I never considered the possible outcome of placing dirty pots in direct contact with the surface upon which we eat.

As an avid gardener, I know that any number of snails, slugs, and bugs can take up residence in my plants. I've even had a few crawl into my bathtub from the plants that surround it. Yet, I never paused to consider the possibility that they might make their way onto our dinner table.

Similarly, we often make thoughtless choices in our lives. In the verses above, Paul reminds us that we live in a creation marred by sin. The potential for undesirable circumstances is a constant reality. While we can't control the outcome of every situation, we can increase the probability for success by making thoughtful choices. Paul encourages us to slow down, consider our options, and seek God's guidance. Meditating and praying over each decision may cost you time, but your investment will yield rich dividends.

Heavenly Father, thank you for promising to provide wisdom when I ask. So, I ask now that you would grant me wisdom in great measure. As I grow in wisdom, help me make thoughtful decisions that align with your will. Give me the insight to learn from past mistakes and make better decisions in the future. Thank you for showing me what wisdom looks like through the life of Jesus. Help me follow Christ's example by surrendering to your will and serving the people in my life. In Jesus' name, Amen

Personal Reflection

What decisions are you facing in the near future? Make a list of anything on your heart whether it seems life-changing or insignificant. Meditate on each item and consider the possible impact of each decision on your life and the lives of others. Pray for God's guidance and ask him to show you the best path forward.

_____

_____

_____

_____

_____

_____

_____

_____

_____

_____

_____

_____

Day 37

Escargot Kitty

Growing up, we always had animals in our home—dogs, cats, birds, hamsters, and even the occasional rabbit or squirrel. When I was a teenager, we adopted the most adorable, fluffy, orange kitten. She had a lively, sweet disposition, but some very unfortunate habits. Our adorable kitten loved to eat slugs.

My mother, a Master Gardener, had cultivated plentiful vegetation and rich soil around the perimeter of our home, an optimal environment for slugs and snails. Also known as gastropods, the slimy creatures oozed toward our yard in droves. The well-nourished, plus-sized gastropods would emerge from hiding in the evenings and early mornings, which are also prime times for animals to go outside and do their business. So, while the slimy pests littered the ground, our kitten would dart from slug to slug, slurping up her favorite snack.

At first, the behavior was humorous. Our kitty would smack the gooey snacks like she had a mouth full of peanut butter. The slime would coat her mouth as well as the soft fur around her mouth, nose, and chin. We quickly grew weary of cleaning the sticky residue from her face, and hoped she would grow out of the habit. As she continued to grow, however, she simply ate increasing quantities of slugs, and we realized our hope was in vain.

I wasn't aware at the time, but eating raw snails and slugs is actually very dangerous. The pests harbor parasites that can be deadly for animals. Further, gastropods absorb pesticides such as weed killer and insect repellant, which are harmful to any animal who ingests the slimy creatures.

Unfortunately, our kitty didn't live long enough to develop any maladies as a result of her disgusting dietary habits. The cat met a tragic end one day when she ran out of the house and underneath a car.

The story is unfortunate on multiple levels. Perhaps God spared our kitty from painful and prolonged suffering via parasite by allowing her a quick death. We simply don't know. We may never understand why God allows awful things to happen. We may never know why he allows a loved one to pass prematurely. We may never comprehend the loss of a job or the end of a relationship.

In the Bible, Job is the quintessential example of someone who endures unexplainable suffering. When the wrecked shell of a man questions God, the Father takes Job on a whirlwind tour. Instead of providing answers, God shows Job the magnitude of his work in the universe.

As Job begins to comprehend the vast scope of God's power, his questions begin to seem insignificant. When Job's revelatory experience draws to a close, he repents to God:

Then Job replied to the Lord:
"I know that you can do anything,
and no one can stop you.
You asked, 'Who is this that questions my wisdom
with such ignorance?'
It is I—and I was talking about things I knew
nothing about,
things far too wonderful for me.
You said, 'Listen and I will speak!
I have some questions for you,
and you must answer them.'

I had only heard about you before,
but now I have seen you with my own eyes.
I take back everything I said,
and I sit in dust and ashes to show my repentance."

Job 42:1–6

In the end, Job understands that he doesn't need to understand. He repents for his lack of trust and reaffirms his faith in God's sovereignty.

Because we serve a God who is infinitely powerful, yet also infinitely loving, we can trust his sovereign hand in our lives. Hard things will happen, we will have seasons of mourning, and we may never know why. Our Lord sees all of time and is preparing for a future of which we have no inkling. Even when you and I don't understand, he is powerful enough to handle it anyway.

Heavenly Father, thank you for being a close friend, a powerful creator, and a loving sustainer. I repent of doubting you in seasons of hardship and mourning. Give me greater faith in your love and your power. I pray that my own example of unwavering faith would encourage other people in my life to trust you more. Give me the fortitude to persevere in my purpose even when life is difficult. In Jesus' name, Amen

Personal Reflection

Prayerfully evaluate your responses to loss and hardship in the past. Do seasons of suffering shake your faith or do you trust God throughout your trials? Does hardship incapacitate you or do you persevere by relying on God's sustaining grace. Ask God to show you what you can learn from your past struggles so that you can respond with greater faith in the future.

Day 38
The Devil's Workshop — Part 1

I'm sure you've heard the saying, "an idle mind is the devil's workshop." Although the maxim technically comes from Scripture, the phrase reflects a very old, very bad translation of Proverbs 16:27. The verse is better translated, "Scoundrels create trouble; their words are a destructive blaze," which has nothing to do with an idle mind.

The detriment of idleness isn't taught by Proverbs 16:27 or explicitly stated in any Bible verse, but the principle is implicitly found in many biblical passages. We'll look at one such passage in a moment, but first I'd like to share one of my husband's rare moments of foolishness.

We all know that teenagers aren't characterized by wise choices, especially teen boys. Although Wesley was an uncharacteristically mature and well-behaved young man, even he was led astray by an idle mind.

One weekend, Wesley and his friends were having a sleepover. They were too young to drive but too old to be content sitting around the house. As the night wore on, their idleness became fertile ground for a poor decision. The boys decided to go for a walk in the middle of the night. I'm not sure why, but they walked right into the "bad" part of town, the neighborhood in which shootings and major crimes regularly occurred. Fortunately, they didn't encounter any danger during their late-night stroll. They wouldn't even have gotten caught had they not brought home a souvenir—a stop sign that they "found on the ground."

My point is that idleness elicited an unwise course of action even from my rule-following, law-abiding husband. Those of us who are prone to push boundaries and challenge the status quo are even more susceptible to making poor choices when we are idle.

King David himself made a string of horrible decisions that began in a season of idleness. According to 2 Samuel 11:1–3, "In the spring of the year, when kings normally go out to war, David sent Joab and the Israelite army to fight the Ammonites. . . . However, David stayed behind in Jerusalem. Late one afternoon, after his midday rest, David got out of bed and was walking on the roof of the palace. As he looked out over the city, he noticed a woman of unusual beauty taking a bath."

David's inactivity produced disastrous outcomes. Instead of going to war as was expected of the king, David stayed home and sent someone else. Rather than leading his army, David was lounging around taking naps. David had gotten a little too comfortable with his posh, kingly life. Because he was the highest authority in the kingdom, he could do whatever he wanted, and apparently that included doing nothing at all.

Unfortunately, David had forgotten that there was an authority even greater than himself. Instead of diligently serving the Lord, he had begun serving himself. If you continue reading in 2 Samuel 11, you'll see that David's self-service resulted in abuse of power, adultery, murder, and the death of his child. His dishonorable actions likely also caused long term harm by damaging his credibility, destabilizing his family, and weakening his kingdom.

We can take preemptive action by offering every second of our time to God. I don't mean praying and serving every waking moment, but rather, making choices that honor the Lord in times of work and times of rest. Let's give God the best we have to have in season, out of season, and everything in between.

Lord, thank you for providing me with the wisdom to make wise decisions. Forgive me for choosing to engage in activities that I know are outside of your will. Help me faithfully follow you and serve you rather than succumbing to idleness. Show me how to honor you in moments of service as well as moments of inactivity. Give me a desire to live according to your holy guidelines for my life. Thank you for loving me and forgiving me even when I am unlovely. In Jesus' name, Amen

Personal Reflection

Prayerfully meditate on your moments of inactivity. Are you inactive because, like David, you are avoiding your duties? Or are your periods of idleness healthy opportunities for rest? Whether you are taking a needed respite or evading responsibilities, consider how you can honor God with your time more fully. Write down your thoughts and we will revisit them tomorrow.

_____

_____

_____

_____

_____

_____

_____

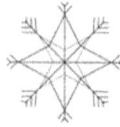

Day 39
The Devil's Workshop — Part 2

Yesterday we talked about honoring God in moments of idleness. The way in which we manage idleness can have just as great an impact on our lives as moments of activity. Our loving father knows that idle minds and hands create an opportunity for the Adversary to wreak havoc in our lives. When David shirked his responsibilities, he ended up sleeping with the neighbor's wife. Yet, he was "a man after God's own heart" (1 Samuel 13:14).

I also mentioned that when Wesley and his friends were bored, they broke the rules, placed themselves in jeopardy, and stole government property. Since Wesley is the most honorable person I know, I can confidently say that even the best among us are susceptible to stupidity caused by inactivity.

While most of us struggle with being overly busy rather than being inactive, our busyness can sometimes foster unhealthy periods of idleness. When we allow ourselves to become exhausted, we are more likely to choose unhealthy escapes when we finally get an idle moment.

I suspect that David may have experienced something similar. He had spent years serving Saul while the king's mental health deteriorated. When David was finally forced to flee in fear of his life, he spent many more years on the run in the Judean wilderness. After Saul died and David became king, he spent another lengthy period at war with the enemies of Israel. When David finally achieved stability for himself and his kingdom, I believe he was mentally, emotionally, and physically exhausted.

While our Father is honored by diligence, perseverance, and hard work, he desires that we develop healthy rhythms of life. Paul exhorts, "Work willingly at whatever you do, as though you were working for the Lord rather than for people," (Colossians 3:23). Working for the Lord entails using our time efficiently, laboring with joy, operating with excellence, AND making time for rest. Our Father desires that we serve him with health and longevity, and we can only accomplish the fullness of his purpose when we foster a healthy balance between periods of work and rest.

God calls us to work diligently while also developing habits that refresh our souls. When we honor Him with our time, he provides an abundant life (John 10:10). Whether we work in an office, a factory, a retail store, a church, or at home, we honor him by cultivating balance. Let's work hard, play hard, and rest well to the glory of God!

Heavenly Father, thank you for sending Jesus to show me how to live a balanced life. Give me the diligence and perseverance to work hard without giving up. Help me serve you with excellence in my home, workplace, and church. Provide strength when I grow weary and teach me how to refresh my soul in healthy ways. I repent of seeking avenues of refreshing that dishonor you. Guide me as I seek to develop healthy rhythms of work and rest. In Jesus' Name, Amen

Personal Reflection

Yesterday, you meditated on how you might honor God with your time more fully. Consider our discussion from today, and look over your notes from yesterday. Prayerfully ask God whether he would have you honor him by working with greater diligence and excellence, implementing godly strategies for refreshing your soul, or finding a healthier balance between periods of work and rest. Write down a couple of strategies you can implement to better honor God, balance your life, and care for your soul.

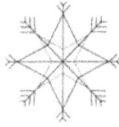

Day 40
Shammah's Stand

Today, I would like to introduce you to Shammah, one of David's "mighty men." The mighty men were 30 elite warriors who protected the king and led the Israelite army. Within this group of 30, three men stood above the rest, and Shammah was one of those three. Although the authors of Scripture give him only a few lines, his actions speak volumes about his character. According to 2 Samuel 23:11–12, "One time the Philistines gathered at Lehi and attacked the Israelites in a field full of lentils. The Israelite army fled, but Shammah held his ground in the middle of the field and beat back the Philistines. So, the Lord brought about a great victory."

Shammah was an elite warrior, and the men he led were battle hardened soldiers. His military force was not composed of unskilled farmers but trained fighters. Yet, for unexplained reasons, they fled in fear while Shammah stood his ground.

Shammah's boldness represents more than confidence in his own fighting skills. His unwillingness to allow the Philistine army to occupy Israelite territory speaks to his faith in God's promises. The Lord had entrusted the land to his people, and thus, defending the land was akin to a defense of his faith. Shammah's faith was so strong that he was willing to stake his life upon God's promises.

My favorite aspect of the narrative is Shammah's name, which is both appropriate and ironic. Shammah means "one who is abandoned, desolate, or deserted." Although he was, indeed, deserted when his soldiers left him standing alone in the middle of the field, Shammah wasn't really abandoned or alone at all. Shammah knew that the number of fighters at his back didn't matter because God was with him. Further, because Shammah took a stand for the Lord, God used him to accomplish a miraculous victory.

Perhaps you feel alone, deserted, and desolate, but God is with you. When you courageously stand for God, even if you feel outnumbered and overpowered, God can work powerful feats through your faith.

Heavenly Father, thank you for never abandoning or forsaking me. Give me the courage to stand against your enemies with confidence. Empower me to do great things upon your behalf. Help me seize opportunities to defend my faith in a gracious and loving way that draws people to you. Forgive me for times when I've withdrawn in fear instead of standing strong in faith. Give me the discernment to recognize the schemes of the enemy and the boldness to refuse to give ground. In Jesus' name, Amen

Personal Reflection

Prayerfully consider how you respond when your faith is challenged. Do you boldly defend your faith or compromise in order to avoid conflict? Consider how you can cultivate greater courage to defend your faith boldly and live without compromise.

_____

_____

_____

_____

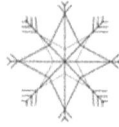

Day 41

Mighty Men

Yesterday, we talked about Shammah, one of King David's mighty men whose name means "abandoned" or "deserted." Although the army of Israel did, indeed, abandon him, Shammah was never truly alone. As Shammah stood in faith, God stood with him and delivered a miraculous victory over the enemy.

In the same chapter, we learn about Eleazar, another of David's elite warriors. Like Shammah, Eliazar refused to flee in the face of overwhelming odds. When the army of Israel retreated in fear, Eleazar stood his ground and struck down Philistines until his hand cramped around his sword. Once again, the Lord rewarded a faithful warrior with a great victory (2 Samuel 23:9–10).

The last of David's elite warrior triumvirate was Jashobeam, the mightiest of the three. The author of 2 Samuel informs us that on one occasion Jashobeam "used his spear to kill 800 enemy warriors in a single battle," (2 Samuel 23:8).

The bravery and faith of Shammah, Eliazar, and Jashobeam provide a stark contrast to David's subsequent actions. Shortly after the miraculous success of his warriors, King David ordered a census of Israel, the purpose of which was to number available fighting men. The request exposed a glaring lack of spiritual awareness in David since God had just empowered three of David's warriors to defeat overwhelming numbers of foes. The Lord had unequivocally shown David that no enemy force could overcome his people while they remained faithful. Yet, despite God's overt display of faithfulness and power, David made the bizarre choice to order a census.

David was a man after God's own heart, yet he made a lot of mistakes. God could have white-washed David's sins and portrayed David in a more virtuous light throughout Scripture. However, to omit David's mistakes would also erase what, I believe, makes him a man after God's heart.

Each time David sinned, he confessed, repented, and returned to God. According to 2 Samuel 24:10, "After he had taken the census, David's conscience began to bother him. And he said to the Lord, "I have sinned greatly by taking this census. Please forgive my guilt, Lord, for doing this foolish thing."" After David repented, he contritely accepted his consequences.

The application I would like to highlight today is that we must take responsibility for our mistakes. If a man after God's own heart can make such egregious errors, we'll probably make a few of our own. If the Father can forgive a man who committed adultery and murder, and whose mistakes impacted an entire nation, he can certainly forgive you and I. Let's learn to confess our shortcomings without delay and stand in Faith with our Father.

Heavenly Father, thank you for covering each of my mistakes with your mercy and grace. Give me the wisdom to recognize when I've made a mistake and the courage to admit it. Help me learn from my mistakes so that I don't repeat them. Empower me to stand upon my faith so that I'm not intimidated by the schemes of the enemy or tempted by his snares. Open my eyes so that I see what you are doing around me and walk in your will. In Jesus' name, Amen

Day 41

Personal Reflection

Make a point of recognizing and acknowledging your mistakes today. Practice apologizing and repenting instead of making excuses.

_____

_____

_____

_____

_____

_____

_____

_____

_____

_____

_____

_____

_____

_____

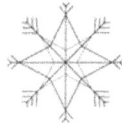

Day 42
Secret Skittles

My older son, Asher, is basically a clone of my husband, Wesley. Both men are tall and slender, with fair complexions and red hair. They are even-tempered, prudent, and respectful of authority. Yet, just as Wesley once participated in an uncharacteristic display of foolishness, Asher likewise entered a period of stealthy disobedience. His secret rebellion was so well-hidden that we didn't find out about it until many years later.

During a routine dentist visit when Asher was around the age of five, we discovered that he'd developed six cavities. I was both shocked and baffled. I couldn't understand how Asher's teeth could have deteriorated so significantly in the six months since our previous visit. I was certain that Asher's dental hygiene had been exceptional. Dr. Doug, our dentist and close friend, knew we took excellent care of our teeth and was likewise puzzled. We were forced to conclude that Asher simply had bad teeth.

Although the cavities afflicted only baby teeth, a series of dentist visits was required to clean the decay and cap the teeth. Since Dr. Doug wasn't a pediatric dentist and Asher's decay was extensive, he recommended a colleague. Our temporary dentist was excellent, but Asher was petrified about going to an unfamiliar place, meeting an unknown person, and facing an uncomfortable procedure. Although I was sympathetic, I was more petrified by the exorbitant cost of the recurring visits.

As time wore on, Asher's marred baby teeth were replaced by healthy adult teeth. Wesley and I forgot about the tooth travails, and Asher's sin remained hidden. Nearly ten years after the cavities, he finally admitted culpability. He confessed that each night after everyone went to sleep, he would sit in bed, play video games, and eat Skittles. He couldn't remember how long the period of sneaky snacking continued, but clearly it was long enough for six cavities to develop.

Like Asher, the nation of Israel faced harsh consequences for their sin. As God's people approached the Promised Land, Moses warned, "If you do not [obey], behold, you have sinned against the Lord, and be sure that your sin will find you out," (Numbers 32:23). Indeed, their disobedience eventually led to persecution, captivity, and destruction.

Asher learned the hard way that sin is never innocuous. Even if the sin remains secret for a time, symptoms and side-effects soon become apparent. Although Asher thought his secret snack sessions were harmless, they created problems for the whole family. Sin creates a blast radius that impacts every person in the proximity. As the transgressor faces fallout at the epicenter of the blast, loved ones also get pelted by shrapnel.

Asher, in the epicenter of his disaster, was forced to undergo frightening dental procedures. Wesley and I, facing the shrapnel of Asher's disobedience, incurred a massive drain on our time and financial resources.

When Asher finally confessed, we forgave him without reservation. In fact, we've enjoyed many a good laugh imagining our well-behaved, rule-following son sneaking late-night Skittles. I'm even thankful that he provided such an excellent illustration about secret sin.

Father, thank you for forgiving my sins—past, present, and future. Give me a greater desire to resist temptation and live with integrity. Help me walk in purity even when no one is watching. Establish my love for you so firmly that sin can't take root in my heart. I pray that instead of being tempted to sin, I would be repulsed by behaviors that dishonor you and harm my loved ones. In Jesus' name, Amen.

Personal Reflections

Prayerfully and honestly self-assess your hidden life. Are you allowing any secret sins to cause decay in your spiritual life? Are you the same person in public as in private? Ask God to help you identify one or more steps you can take to live with greater integrity. Write down your thoughts so you can revisit them tomorrow.

_____

_____

_____

_____

_____

_____

_____

_____

_____

_____

Day 42

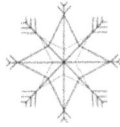

Day 43
Undercover Nachos

Yesterday, we talked about Asher's secret sin—the late-night Skittles that caused six cavities. Because I'm a good and fair parent, I'll tell you about Abel's shameful snack as well. Although his transgression didn't lead to any long-term consequences, he did face parental discipline.

To set the scene, let me explain that my boys share a playroom. In years past, the room contained mostly toys. Now that the boys are older, the room houses a large television, a computer, and various videogame consoles. Although the carpet is already stained past the point of no return, Wesley and I don't allow food in the room to protect the electronics and furniture. The rule has existed since we moved into the house nearly ten years ago, so both boys are well-familiar with the playroom food prohibition.

As the playroom adjoins the kitchen, the food ban is no great affliction. One can comfortably sit at the kitchen table while watching the playroom TV. For Abel, however, that wasn't enough.

On the day his sin was exposed, Abel arrived home from school just before I arrived home from work. Not realizing I was near the house, Abel had just enough time to make a big plate of nachos, turn on his favorite show, and relax on the playroom daybed with the nachos balanced on his stomach. To avoid detection, he shut the doors and then dug into his snack. Unfortunately for Abel, the sound of the television and the closed doors prevented him from hearing my arrival.

Knowing the boys were home, I approached the playroom and opened the door to say "hello." My greeting turned into a gasp as I viewed the scene. In a singular moment, I saw a look of panic on Abel's face and a plate of nachos on his stomach. Simultaneously, Abel jerked the bedcovers across his nacho-laden body in a futile attempt to hide the illicit snack. I struggled to respond, balancing on a razor's edge between hysterical laughter and unbridled anger. Abel's blatant disobedience was infuriating, but his panicked cover-up was hilarious. I couldn't help but think of 1 John 2:28, "And now, dear children, remain in fellowship with Christ so that when he returns, you will be full of courage and not shrink back from him in shame." Instead of greeting me with his customary bear-hug, Abel's actions caused him to recoil in fear and shame.

Once I decided upon an appropriate course of action, Abel accepted his discipline with dignity. He was caught red-handed, or rather greasy-nacho-handed, and he knew that correction was unavoidable. What he failed to realize, like every other kid in the world, was that I didn't want to punish him. I want our time together to be full of joy. Yet, if my boys place themselves in situations that require discipline, they will receive discipline.

Wesley and I want the best for my kids. We create reasonable rules and healthy boundaries for their benefit. Teaching our boys to obey the rules equips them to live in joy, walk with integrity, and avoid the negative consequences of sin. For example, the playroom food ban ensures that the space remains functional, safe, and fun for our boys and their friends. Bringing food into the room has the potential to ruin electronics, spread mold, and damage furniture, all of which have occurred even without food present.

Abel still feels ashamed of his poor behavior even though the disciplinary measures are long past and quite forgotten. Our Father, like a loving parent, wants to spare us those psychological consequences, as well as the tangible ones that often accompany bad decisions. Paul exhorts, "For freedom Christ set us free; therefore stand firm and never again subject yourself to a to a yoke of slavery," (Galatians 5:1, my translation). Even though sin may seem enticing in the moment, disobedience only leads to disappointment, discord, and destruction. Jesus sacrificed himself to give us freedom from the physical, relational, emotional, and spiritual fallout. Although his grace is sufficient to wash away our shame and forgive every sin, sometimes we can't seem to forgive ourselves. Fortunately, God equips his children to make wise choices and proactively avoid the spiral of shame. Let's resist the naughty nachos as we walk in freedom and stand in faith.

Father, thank you for providing freedom and forgiveness in abundance. Give me the self-discipline to resist temptation and the wisdom to avoid bad decisions. Empower me to walk in freedom and grow in faith. Help me also grow in compassion toward those who might be in bondage to sin. Show me how I can use the lessons I've learned from my own mistakes to help others overcome their struggles. Help me continually grow in integrity so that when you return I'll be full of courage and joy rather than fear and shame. In Jesus' name, Amen.

Personal Reflection

First, re-read your notes from yesterday in the light of this question: If your Savior returned today, would you feel joyfully courageous or fearfully ashamed? If you feel joyful about the return of Christ, write down a list of habits that help you maintain integrity, grow spiritually, and walk in freedom. Consider whether you should bolster your list with any new practices, revise any old ones, or reestablish any disciplines in which you've grown lax. If the thought of Christ's return evokes fear or shame in your heart, read Ephesians

1:4–8 and pray the verses over yourself. Consider memorizing the
verses or displaying them in a prominent place.

**Scan the QR
code for
passages of
Scripture**

_____

_____

_____

_____

_____

_____

_____

_____

_____

_____

_____

_____

Day 44

Dangerous Dessert

Yesterday we talked about Abel's illicit playroom nachos and the undesirable consequences of sin. Today, I'd like to jump much further back in time to a different snack in a different playroom.

Allow me to set the scene. In the Fall volume of devotionals, I introduced you to my first schnauzer, a feisty little girl named Schmutzie. When I adopted her, I was still living at home with my parents and dating Wesley.

On the day in question, Wesley and I had gone out for ice cream then returned home to play video games. Since I couldn't hold a dessert and a game controller at the same time, I sat my cup of chocolate ice cream nearby on the floor. My faithful pup, still only a few months old, sat happily by my side.

As Wesley and I became engrossed in our game, I promptly forgot about my ice cream and my puppy. At some point, we took a break and discovered Schmutzie neck deep in ice cream. Similar to my inner conflict over Abel's nachos cover-up, I was torn between hysterical laughter and intense fear. Schmutzie's entire head was inside the ice cream cup and covered in sticky chocolate. My little girl had eaten nearly the entire cup of ice cream despite full-body shivers from the cold (and sugary chocolate).

Although Schmutzie's chocolate-covered head and cold shivers were adorable, I knew she was in true danger. Chocolate contains chemicals that can lead to seizure, heart arrhythmia, dehydration, respiratory distress, and death in dogs. Considering the sugar and caffeine in addition to the chocolate, I'm lucky that Schmutzie didn't have a heart attack, fall into a diabetic coma, or simply keel over dead. On the contrary, once we got her clean and warm, Schmutzie was absolutely fine.

I would never have harmed my pup intentionally, but my careless actions could have resulted in devastating consequences. Despite my fierce affection for Schmutzie, my negligence caused inadvertent harm.

As imperfect human beings, we often harm people we love due to carelessness or neglect. Our attentive Heavenly Father, on the other hand, zealously watches over his children. The prophet Ezekiel recounts the Lord's promise to care for his people.

For this is what the Sovereign Lord says: "I myself will search and find my sheep. I will be like a shepherd looking for his scattered flock. I will find my sheep and rescue them from all the places where they were scattered on that dark and cloudy day. I will bring them back home to their own land of Israel from among the peoples and nations. I will feed them on the mountains of Israel and by the rivers and in all the places where people live. Yes, I will give them good pastureland on the high hills of Israel. There they will lie down in pleasant places and feed in the lush pastures of the hills. I myself will tend my sheep and give them a place to lie down in peace, says the Sovereign Lord. I will search for my lost ones who strayed away, and I will bring them safely home again. I will bandage the injured and strengthen the weak. But I

will destroy those who are fat and powerful."
Ezekiel 34:11–16

The Father actively searches for his sheep and rescues them even when they wander away. When he gathers them home, he not only meets their basic needs, but provides abundant sustenance, pleasant places to live, and safe places to sleep. He heals the injured, strengthens the weak, and destroys the enemy.

God not only models zealous protection and provision, but equips us to do the same for those we love.[2] Although you and I will never master the level of care God provides, we can emulate his example by giving close attention to the people in our life. Rather than being focused on self, distracted by responsibilities, or consumed with work, we can cultivate a habit of prioritizing people. Although we would never purposely harm the ones we love, our distraction can leave them exposed to the fiery darts of the Enemy. Let's turn off the television, put down the electronics, and spend some quality time with our people.

Father, thank you for modeling sacrificial love and authentic care for people. Help me learn from your example as I seek to protect the people I love. Give me the self-discipline to eliminate distractions in order to prioritize others. Guide me as I care for my friends and family, and teach me to love them well. Grow my spiritual discernment so that I can be sensitive to the needs of my loved ones and serve them accordingly. Thank you for placing people in my life who likewise minister to my soul. In Jesus name, Amen.

---

[2] While selfless sacrifice and unconditional love please God, he never condones abuse. If any of your relationships are characterized by manipulation, exploitation, or violence, immediately seek professional help.

Personal Reflection

Prayerfully meditate on relationships with close friends and family. Consider how you might better care for your loved ones. As you reflect, organize your thoughts around three "P"s. How can you be more *proactive* about caring for loved ones? How can you better *prioritize* your people in such a way that fosters relational health and spiritual growth? How can you *pray* effectively for the needs and concerns of your friends and family? Write down a few thoughts corresponding to each category.

_____

_____

_____

_____

_____

_____

_____

_____

_____

_____

_____

_____

_____

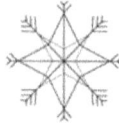

Day 45
Senile Schnauzer

Yesterday we talked about Schmutzie's dangerous dessert and meditated on how we might better care for those we love. Today, we'll focus on how God cares for us as we fast forward from Schmutzie's puppy stage to a harrowing occurrence in her senior years.

When Schmutzie was nearly 14 years old, our family moved into a new home. Sadly, my aging pup was starting to grow senile and didn't adapt well to the move. Schmutzie couldn't find her food bowl, her dog house, or her usual nap spots, although her schnauzer sense of adventure remained strong. Given the slightest opportunity, she would sneak away to explore the new neighborhood.

One particular morning, we couldn't find Schmutzie. We searched the house and the yard. We drove our cars around the neighborhood and shouted her name out the window. For the entire day, Schmutzie was nowhere to be found. I was worried sick trying not to panic over the array of worst-case scenarios swirling through my mind.

As twilight encroached, I decided to search our house and yard once more. I methodically began to open every door and ransack every closet. As a last resort, I even searched the guest room, which was unoccupied, unused, and closed shut. To my great relief, Schmutzie had found her way inside. Apparently, someone had entered and exited the room without knowing that Schmutzie had followed and been shut inside. Beyond the oddity of finding her in a closed and unused room, the strangest aspect of the entire situation was that she hadn't barked, scratched, or lifted a paw to help us help her.

The scenario brings to mind a verse from 2 Chronicles: "The eyes of the Lord search the whole earth in order to strengthen those whose hearts are fully committed to him," (2 Chronicles 16:9a). Our Father is searching throughout creation for his children, eager to come to their aid. Our God is looking for people who desire a relationship with him, people who need hope, and people who are lost. Our Father is searching for you because he wants to meet your needs.

Let me be clear that the searching activity of God doesn't imply he can't find you. Our Father isn't fumbling around, clueless, as when I was searching for my elderly dog. Rather, the verse indicates that God comes to the aid of those who desire a relationship with him. If we don't want him in our lives, God respects our wishes and won't barge through the door. Yet, as soon as we request his aid, invite his presence, and accept his love, he is watching and waiting to come to the rescue.

Sometimes, like Schmutzie, we get lost and confused. Maybe we are stuck in one spot, paralyzed by fear or disillusioned with life. Maybe we feel so hopeless or powerless that we don't even cry out to our Father. Alternately, perhaps we aren't in a season of trial, but we've been trying to navigate life without the presence and power of God. What a tragedy if we stayed stuck, alone, and away from his presence, ignoring his love simply because we never invited him into our life. He is watching and waiting for your call!

Lord, thank you for your watchful protection over my life. Thank you for coming to my aid, strengthening me, and meeting my needs. I repent of ignoring your presence and trying to do life on my own. Teach me to have a heart that is fully committed to you so that I can draw upon your strength without hesitation. Replace my fear with joy and my confusion with confidence. Grant a greater measure of your presence and power in my life. Help me walk in the fullness of your blessing so that I can be a blessing to others. In Jesus' name, Amen.

Personal Reflection

Prayerfully reflect on your life as a whole as well as the various pursuits that fill your time. Do you routinely spend time with God, request his guidance, and draw upon his strength? Do you invite him to be part of every area of your life or do you keep some doors closed? Are you allowing him to sustain you through struggles or are you suffering in silence? Ask God to help you open any doors that have been closed to his presence and cry out for a greater measure of his strength.

_____

_____

_____

_____

_____

_____

_____

_____

_____

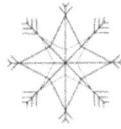

Day 46
Traumatic Bird Injury

One lovely morning, I arrived at the home of my friend Lisa. Just prior to my arrival, a dove had flown into one of her closed windows and fallen to the patio. If you've never experienced this phenomenon, birds sometimes fail to notice window glass and collide with the transparent surface. Usually, they'll recover after momentary disorientation. Our dove did not.

As Lisa and I stood looking out the window, we desperately wanted to help the bird in some way. However, we knew there was nothing we could do. The dove had clearly incurred a traumatic brain injury. I'll spare you a description and simply say that we both had nightmares about the condition of the bird. Fortunately, the poor creature soon passed away and suffered no more.

You and I often feel helpless in the face of suffering and sickness, just as Lisa and I felt standing before the injured bird. We want to ease the pain of others, but we don't know how. Our words seem inadequate and our actions feel futile. We feel helpless because, in truth, there is sometimes little we can do to alleviate the pain and suffering of others.

Paul suggests a course of action that is, perhaps, the best gift we can offer people who are hurting. In Romans 12:15, the apostle says, "Be happy with those who are happy, and weep with those who weep." Whether loved ones are celebrating success or mourning loss, they need love and support. Simply being present in difficult moments sends a message more powerful than words can say.

Although the injured dove probably wasn't comforted by Lisa and I standing by the window, your presence can be a soothing balm to others. Your care brings greater comfort than powerful painkillers and sympathetic speeches. Next time you feel helpless, remember the power of simply being present.

Lord, thank you for your constant presence in my life. Help me to reflect your selfless love as I care for others. Give me greater empathy for those who are hurting and greater sensitivity to their needs. I repent of avoiding people who are suffering because I feel helpless or uncomfortable. Teach me to put aside my own discomfort as I spend time with those who are sick or suffering. Provide opportunities for me to share your care and kindness. In Jesus' name, Amen.

Personal Reflection

Consider calling or visiting someone in your life who is sick or suffering. Talk with them, sit with them, pray with them, or simply let them know you care.

_____

_____

_____

_____

_____

_____

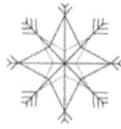

Day 47
An Odd Bird

I think of birds as God's confetti. I imagine our Lord crafting the avian species with a twinkle in his eye and a smile on his face. The vast array of shapes, sizes, and hues add cheer and color to our environment. The variety of behaviors add joviality and majesty to our world.

Some birds, however, are more bizarre than others. We've already discussed the male bird of paradise who comically tidies up his living space before dancing to attract a mate. Other species, such as peacocks and eagles, are more regal and stately. Yet others, though less visually striking, demonstrate phenomenal abilities. Hawks and falcons, for example, can reach speeds over 200 miles per hour!

Even species considered unappealing perform valuable functions. Vultures dispose of rotting carcasses and keep the ecosystem healthy. As they consume carrion, the microbiome of their digestive system kills harmful microorganisms. Then, the antibacterial properties of their waste further prevent the spread of disease-causing microorganisms.

Considering the remarkable variety among birds, we simply can't identify one species as better than the rest. We may favor the appearance of some birds or appreciate the skill of others, but no single trait ranks one species above the others. Each adds beauty and distinctiveness to the world's ecosystem in one way or another.

Yet, in the ecosystem of human culture, we tend to rank people according to a list of desirable traits—sometimes consciously and sometimes unconsciously. These unwritten traits are culturally determined and often arbitrary. In fact, from one culture to the next, desirable attributes can vary wildly.

If you and I desire a healthy mental and spiritual life, we must not base our self-worth on a set of arbitrary standards. When we view our appearance and ability through the standards of our culture, we typically come up short. As a result, we try to conform ourselves to whatever traits are popular in our day, time, and locale.

In Romans 2, Paul warns against conforming to culture. He exhorts, "Don't copy the behavior and customs of this world, but let God transform you into a new person by changing the way you think," (Romans 12:2).

Paul cautions Christ followers against conforming to any standards other than those set by God. What if, instead of conforming to culture, we valued the unique characteristics we bring to God's creation and human culture? When we conform, we deprive the world of our best traits and unique gifts.

From the avian world alone, we can see that our Father loves diversity and variety. There are plenty of odd birds in the animal kingdom, and each is expertly crafted by the Father. In a similar manner, God created each of us with expert care. Even better, he continues to transform us as we embrace our design. We'll delve more deeply into this topic tomorrow, but for now, remember that God doesn't make mistakes—he makes masterpieces.

Father, thank you for creating me with intentionality and care. Forgive me for considering myself worthless when you have made me worthy. Give me the wisdom to embrace my created design without conforming to my culture. Teach me to evaluate my strengths and weaknesses according to your standards. Help me understand how you can work through my unique design, even through traits that I consider weaknesses. I ask you to provide opportunities for me to help others see their worth and value in your eyes. In Jesus' Name, Amen

Personal Reflection

Make a list of traits, skills, and behaviors you like about yourself. Acknowledge each as a gift from God and submit them to him. Meditate on how each can be used to bring him glory.

_____

_____

_____

_____

_____

_____

_____

_____

_____

_____

_____

_____

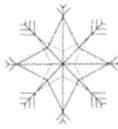

Day 48

More Odd Birds

Yesterday we discussed the diverse assortment of birds created by our Father. From beautiful to mundane, each species has unique characteristics. Even birds that seem inferior have value in their own way.

Some species exhibit remarkable intellect while others are as dumb as the proverbial rock. Ravens, parrots, and crows boast the capacity for thinking, reasoning, and even the ability to mimic speech. Conversely, ostriches and owls exhibit subpar intelligence. Both have oversized eyes, which leave little skull space for the brain. Yet, their mental deficiencies are mediated by physical prowess and other strengths. Owls are exceptional hunters who provide eco-friendly pest control by culling the rodent and insect population. Ostriches, on the other hand, are exceptional at avoiding predators. Equipped with long legs, the ostrich can run at speeds up to nearly 50 miles per hour. If a predator manages to catch up, the bird can use its powerful legs to defend itself with enough force to kill.

While humanity is not as diverse as the avian kingdom, we likewise exhibit variety from person to person and culture to culture. As individuals, we can be tempted to camouflage our distinctiveness by conforming to our environment. However, as we read yesterday, Paul cautions against this trap. He further instructs, "Be honest in your evaluation of yourselves, measuring yourselves by the faith God has given us," (Romans 12:2–3). Instead of evaluating our worth by worldly standards and conforming to culture, God calls us to embrace our identity in Christ and evaluate ourselves in the light of our faith.

For the most part, our self-evaluation takes one of three avenues. First, you may feel like an outsider and deem your worth subpar. Yet, if you sometimes feel like an odd bird, you aren't alone. Rather than berating yourself for falling short in the eyes of the world, you can express gratitude for your unique design. Alternatively, you might consider yourself an "average joe" with little to offer that is unique or exciting. If this is the case, you should remember that not all birds are bright and flashy, but that all are fearfully and wonderfully made by God himself for a purpose. Finally, perhaps you feel stunningly beautiful and capable. Like a tropical bird with brilliant plumage, people may gaze upon you with admiration. You can choose to preen with pride or use your influence to advocate for those at whom no one looks, admires, or appreciates.

Before we conclude, allow me to offer a word of caution. Embracing our identity is not the same as indulging every whim, temptation, and weakness. Succumbing to sin tarnishes our true identity and dirties our unique beauty. Like a bird trapped in an oil slick, self-indulgence saturates our soul and keeps us from God's purpose. Let's follow Paul's advice to align our minds with the principles of God so that we can be transformed and conformed to our created design.

Lord, thank you for creating me with a purpose and for providing everything I need to accomplish it. Teach me to align my thoughts with the truth of your Word and root my identity firmly in Christ. Give me the wisdom to evaluate myself humbly and honestly. I confess that every gift I have is from you and I repent of tolerating sin simply because culture finds it acceptable. Show me how to embrace my design without accepting sin. Empower me to walk out my faith boldly and share the truth with others who are struggling with their identity. In Jesus' name, Amen.

Personal Reflection

Yesterday, you made a list of traits, skills, and behaviors you like about yourself. Today, make a list of things you dislike about yourself. Prayerfully determine whether each item is a sin or struggle that needs to be transformed by God or an aspect of your identity that needs to be embraced or cultivated. Once you are finished, re-read your list from yesterday to encourage yourself!

_____

_____

_____

_____

_____

_____

_____

_____

_____

_____

_____

_____

_____

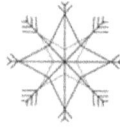

Day 49
Flourishing Ferns

I have a large plot of hardy ferns that grow along one side of my house. They are so resilient that they pop up everywhere. The fronds even emerge in the middle of my dry creek bed, which is filled roughly three feet deep with rocks.

Each winter, the lush ferns completely die off. All the beautiful fronds wither, turn brown, and fall to the ground. That which remains looks like a big pile of dead foliage. However, more is going on than meets the eye.

In winter, the season that is theoretically the most difficult to survive, my ferns grow stronger. During the cold months, the dead plant matter and the hard winter soil insulate the roots of the ferns and keep them from freezing. Beneath their layer of insulation, the roots spread out as they absorb water and grow.

Similarly, God uses periods of dormancy and seasons of adversity to strengthen our spiritual foundations. We may feel like we are spinning our wheels and making little forward progress. Behind the scenes, though, God is nourishing our roots and preparing us to flourish. Paul encourages, "Let your roots grow down into him, and let your lives be built on him. Then your faith will grow strong in the truth you were taught, and you will overflow with thankfulness," (Colossians 2:7).

When our roots become deeply established in the Lord, our lives begin to flourish. Yet, seasons of unseen strengthening are necessary preparation for seasons of fruitfulness. A plant that grows large before the roots are established will topple over and die. Although weak spiritual roots probably won't cause death, they will lead to embarrassing mistakes, unfulfilled expectations, and spiritual disillusionment.

Our Father wants to equip us for a life of fruitfulness and flourishing. Rather than feeling frustration during periods of dormancy, let's thank God for his nourishment. Just as I eagerly anticipate the unfurling fronds in my garden, you can wait upon your next season with joyful expectancy.

Heavenly Father, thank you for loving me in seasons during which I accomplish much for your kingdom and in seasons during which I simply receive your nourishment. Grow my roots deeper in my knowledge of you and your Word. Prepare me to emerge from my current season and bear fruit that nourishes others. Empower me to spread the beauty of the Gospel message as I flourish in the light of your love. In Jesus' Name, Amen

Personal Reflection

Meditate on your current season of life. Are you in a period of dormant preparation or purposeful flourishing? If you are in a season of unseen preparation, cultivate gratitude and fortify your foundation. Thank God for the blessings unique to this season, seek his guidance, and submit to his plan. Write down a few areas of your life in which God is currently helping you grow. If you are in a season of flourishing and outward growth, consider how your life can bear fruit and nourish others to a greater extent. Write down your thoughts below.

_____

_____

_____

Day 49

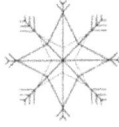

Day 50

Weathering the Storm

In our region of the southeast U.S., changing seasons are accompanied by drastic temperature swings. When fall transitions to winter, the weather might consist of warm breezes one day, and freezing sleet the next. Our Christmas can involve shorts and sunshine or sweaters and snow.

Likewise, our emotions can be as fickle as the weather. Even on our best days, minor annoyances can snowball into simmering anger and disappointments into depression. Even worse, when we are facing legitimate grief or anguish, we can feel stuck in the midst of a storm from which the sun will never emerge.

However, just as the most brutal storm will eventually pass, difficult emotions won't last forever. Even more encouraging, we can't control the weather, but we can take steps to minimize mood swings. When we grow our roots deeper in the Lord, as we talked about yesterday, he provides mental stability and emotional fortitude.

I think Jeremiah, who is often called the "weeping prophet," understood the difficulty of managing emotions. He bemoans the untrustworthy state of the heart, saying, "The human heart is the most deceitful of all things, and desperately wicked. Who really knows how bad it is?" (Jeremiah 17:9). Yet, I think the "weeping prophet" also understood that remaining rooted in the Lord keeps us stable, fruitful, and able to weather every storm. In the verses immediately prior to his statements about the heart, he says, "Blessed are those who trust in the Lord and have made the Lord their hope and confidence. They are like trees planted along a riverbank, with roots that reach deep into the water. Such trees are not bothered by the heat or worried by long months of drought. Their leaves stay green, and they never stop producing fruit," (Jeremiah 17:7–8).

In our lives, we know with certainty that storms will come. We also know with certainty that our Father can shelter us from the elements. Just as he created the sun, wind, and rain, he created the complexity of our emotions. Accordingly, our emotions aren't bad or good, but rather a gauge that provides information about our inner life. When we submit our hearts to the Father and become rooted in him, we can learn from our emotions rather than be driven by them. However, just as trees planted along a riverbank require years to become deeply rooted, we likewise need time to become grounded in God and aware of our emotional tendencies.

Regardless of whether you are just beginning to spread your roots through the fertile soil of faith or you've been growing them deeper and stronger for years, know that your storm will not last. Just as the sun emerges from the clouds after a storm, your "weeping may last through the night, but joy comes with the morning," (Psalm 30:5).

Heavenly Father, thank you for giving me the strength to weather every storm. Give me the desire and diligence to grow my roots more deeply in you so that I'm not tossed about by the wind. Show me how to deal with my emotions in a healthy way. Help me find a balance between avoiding my feelings and allowing them to consume me. Instill joy in my heart that endures even during seasons of grief and hardship. Grow my faith so that my trust in your goodness does not waver even when my emotions do. In Jesus' name, Amen

Personal Reflection

Cultivating emotional self-awareness, especially in a mindset of faith, can help us better process and regulate shifting emotions. Today, begin a practice of identifying your emotional "weather" during your quiet time with God. Don't judge the validity of your emotions, simply acknowledge how you feel and ask your Father to help you understand why you feel this way. Ask God to help you consciously and wisely respond rather than react to what you are feeling. Finally, release the need to control your emotions, remember that you are not defined by them, and reaffirm your faith in your good Father.

_____

_____

_____

_____

_____

_____

_____

_____

_____

_____

_____

_____

Day 51
Drowning in Grief or Anchored In Faith

Yesterday we talked about our emotions, which can be as fickle as the weather. By rooting ourselves in God's sustaining love, we can weather the storms of life with stability and fortitude.

Emotions aren't bad or good, but our response to them can keep us adrift in stormy seas if we don't learn to manage them. Grief, in particular, is an emotion that can be excruciatingly difficult to weather. Mourning a loss, whether that of a loved one, a relationship, or a job, can feel like it consumes every particle of our being. Sometimes grief overtakes us in a flood, sometimes in waves, and sometimes in a light sprinkle that is almost possible to ignore. Yet, even months or years after a loss, grief can arise like a flash flood and catch us unaware.

Instead of drowning in grief, we can choose to root ourselves in God's sustaining love. Otherwise, we will, indeed, be tossed by the waves. James advises, "be sure that your faith is in God alone. Do not waver, for a person with divided loyalty is as unsettled as a wave of the sea that is blown and tossed by the wind," (James 1:6). Through faith, we can remain unmovable and unshakable through the storms of life. However, we must become rooted *before* the waves and winds crash upon our lives. Then, even when we face seasons of grief, we won't be tossed adrift and washed away by the storm.

Both James and Paul provide specific instructions for becoming rooted in our faith. James instructs us to view the storms of life as opportunities for growth and seek God's wisdom to navigate them

(James 1:2–5). Paul advises us to saturate our minds in God's Word. "Then we will no longer be immature like children. We won't be tossed and blown about by every wind of new teaching," (Ephesians 4:14). When we know the truth, the enemy won't be able to knock us into the waves and drown us with his clever lies.

If grief comes upon you like a sudden storm, simply allow your emotions to crest, knowing that the winds and waves will eventually subside. From your deeply rooted dwelling of faith, you'll remain anchored in his love until brighter days.

Lord, thank you for creating me with complex emotions that reflect your character and image. Help me to master my emotions rather than letting them toss me about. Grow my roots so deeply in your love that I'm anchored through every storm. Teach me to view my moments and seasons of grief as opportunities to grow in character and learn perseverance. Help me make wise decisions so that I'm prepared to weather storms when they arise. Increase my desire for spending time in Scripture so that I can discern your truth from the lies of the enemy. In Jesus' name, Amen.

Personal Reflection

Continue cultivating emotional self-awareness today. Once again, identify your emotional "weather." Don't judge the validity of your emotions, simply acknowledge how you feel and ask your Father to help you understand why you feel this way. Ask God to help you consciously and wisely respond rather than react to what you are feeling. Finally, release the need to control your emotions, remember that you are not defined by them, and reaffirm your faith in your Father.

Day 51

Day 52
Snows and Streams

In my region, the likelihood of snow is extremely unpredictable. If meteorologists predict heavy snow, we'll probably get a light dusting. If they predict flurries, we'll probably get several feet. Most years, we have one substantial snow in which the kids can play and build snowmen. However, the snow might occur in early December, late March, or anything in between.

Shockingly, at least for me, snow is a regular occurrence in Israel. Before my first visit, I envisioned the countryside as a flat, dry desert. Upon arrival, I was delighted to experience lush tropics, gorgeous beaches, fertile farmland, rolling hills, and snowy mountains.

The mountainous region of Israel runs parallel to the Mediterranean coastline from the southernmost border of the country and extends into Lebanon in the north. Upon the mountainous peaks, especially the steep northern mountains, snow is a predictable occurrence. The snowmelt in the spring can be depended upon to feed the country's freshwater rivers and provide water for crops. The snow is so predictable that Jeremiah uses it as a metaphor for the faithfulness of God. The prophet rhetorically asks,

> *Does the snow ever disappear from the mountain-*
> *tops of Lebanon?*
> *Do the cold streams flowing from those distant*
> *mountains ever run dry?*

But my people are not so reliable, for they have deserted me;
they burn incense to worthless idols.
They have stumbled off the ancient highways
and walk in muddy paths.
Therefore, their land will become desolate,
a monument to their stupidity.
All who pass by will be astonished
and will shake their heads in amazement.
I will scatter my people before their enemies
as the east wind scatters dust.
And in all their trouble I will turn my back on them
and refuse to notice their distress.

Jeremiah 18:14–17

Just as the mountains of Israel and Lebanon will have snow tipped peaks and deliver life-giving water, our father will always be faithful.

When the people of Israel were learning to follow God, he was as constant as snow falling on mountains and water flowing through springs. Unfortunately, God's people were not as steadfast. Instead of faithfully walking beside the life-giving springs that he provided, they went off course and trudged through the metaphorical mud. Instead of walking in the safety of his provision and protection, they forged their own path right into desolation and humiliation.

I would warrant a guess that for most of us, the tenor of our life is closer to that of the biblical Israelites than that of the Lord. We trudge through our own mud instead of walking beside God's refreshing, sustaining stream. We forget that when we forsake God's path and forge our own, we step outside of his protection and into dangerous terrain. Only later do we limp back to him wounded and malnourished.

Thankfully, our Father will welcome us back into his arms no matter how many detours we take. Further, the more we abide in his presence, the less we want to leave, and the more we take on his character.

Why don't we leave the muddy trails behind and learn from past mistakes? Has walking away from God's will ever yielded the outcome for which we hoped? I don't think so.

Father, thank you for your faithfulness to protect me and provide for my needs. I praise you for forgiving me and refreshing my soul when I make mistakes. I repent of going my own way and stepping outside of your will. Give me the wisdom to learn from my past mistakes so that I can follow you more faithfully. Help me be wary of the schemes and temptations with which the Enemy tries to lead me astray. Give me a greater desire to abide in your presence and reflect your faithfulness. In Jesus' name, Amen.

Personal reflection

Are you currently walking through the mud and taking a detour from God's will in any area of your life? If the answer is "yes," repent and ask God to help you return to his path. If you are unsure, pray and ask God to show you any areas in which you may have stepped outside of his will. Then ask him to lead you back to his life-giving path.

_____

_____

_____

Day 52

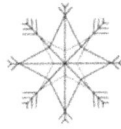

Day 53
Dirty Snow

Yesterday, we compared the erratic winter precipitation in the southeastern U.S. with the faithful mountain snow in northern Israel. While our Father is as faithful as snow on the mountaintops, you and I behave more like unpredictable flurries. As imperfect humans, we tend to detour from God's will, forge our own path, and trudge through the mud. Lest you feel condemned, however, I want to encourage you by discussing God's response to our detours.

First, though, let me tell you more about snow in Alabama. As I mentioned, we only get one or two substantial snows per year, and by "substantial" I mean 3–4 inches. The blanket of snow is deep enough to make snowmen, build snow forts, and sometimes even go sledding if you're industrious.

In years past, my boys loved snow so much that Asher would pray for it every night before bed. When we would finally receive a decent snow, I'd dress the boys in layer upon layer of clothing, along with boots, gloves, hats, and scarves. They would stay outside for hours playing in their winter wonderland.

As the day wore on, however, the winter wonder would turn into muddy misery. Boys would peel off bulky layers and snow would begin to melt. The pristine blanket of white would transform into a muddy brown mire. Frost covered boys would return to the house, track mud across the floors, and leave a trail of damp clothing. As their icy chill wore off, the numbness would turn into pain, wailing, and gnashing of teeth.

I share our snow story to point out that I don't get angry about the aftermath. Although I instruct the boys not to destroy the yard, track mud through the house, or leave clothes on the floor, my yard turns into a soggy mire and my house turns into a muddy mess. Nonetheless, I welcome my boys inside with open arms. I comfort them and cuddle them through the discomfort of thawing out. I clean them up, warm them up, and fill up their bellies with hot chocolate. Then I clean up the mess left in their wake. I know they don't purposefully make a mess. Yet, even if they did, no amount of mess or mud could induce me to turn my boys away.

I have trouble conceptualizing the love of God, which is so much greater than my own love for my boys. Yet I know that if he loves me even more than I love Asher and Abel, he will love me no matter how big of a mess I make, how many times I track through the mud, or how often I wander into the wilderness. I routinely thank God for his continuing faithfulness and claim the words of David in Psalm 40:2, "He lifted me out of the pit of despair, out of the mud and the mire. He set my feet on solid ground and steadied me as I walked along." Let's stick to the steady path and solid ground, abiding in the protection and provision of our Father.

Father, thank you for your faithfulness to protect me and provide for my needs. Thank you for lifting me out of the mud in times when I have gone astray. Give me a desire to walk in consistency and obedience so that I don't get myself stuck in the mud of bad decisions. Help me grasp more fully the depth of your love for me. Fill my heart with such love for you that I have no desire to step outside of your will. In Jesus' name, Amen.

Personal Reflection

Meditate on the multitude of ways that God protects you and provides for you. Write down a few of your favorites below and thank your Father for each one.

tion or through the filter of God's love.

_____

_____

_____

_____

_____

_____

_____

_____

_____

_____

_____

_____

_____

Day 54
This Is the Day

I love the holidays, but winter is not my favorite season. I don't like cold weather. I don't like snow. I don't enjoy winter sports. Once the holidays are past, I'm ready for winter to be over.

Spring flowers, sunny days, and warm breezes nourish my soul. Gardening, swimming, and hiking refresh my spirit. When I'm deprived of so many things that bring me joy, it's hard to stay positive. So, in the wintertime, I have to make an extra effort to see the blessings in each day. According to Psalm 118,

This is the day the Lord has made.
We will rejoice and be glad in it.
You are my God, and I will praise you!
You are my God, and I will exalt you!
Give thanks to the Lord, for he is good!
His faithful love endures forever.
Psalm 118:24, 28–29

Every single day is a gift from God—not just warm days filled with sunshine, but also days that are cold, dark, sad, and hard.

Some days simply require us to exert extra effort to foster the joy of the Lord. We can choose to mope, pout, and despair or we can take strategic steps to stay encouraged. As for me, I take joy in the little things that I enjoy about winter, like peppermint lattes, comfy blankets, warm sweaters, and sitting by the fireplace with family. When I feel an emotional slump encroaching, I list as many blessings as I can think of and thank God for each. Instead of focusing on the things that I don't like about winter, I make a daily decision to shift my focus to the good things God is doing in my life.

The effort is worthwhile because joy is a vital element of our spiritual health. Fostering joy isn't simply about trying to be happier. The joy of the Lord is our strength (Nehemiah 8:10). If we allow ourselves to wallow in misery, we've weakened our soul and created fertile ground for the enemy to sow seeds of deception and destruction. I don't know about you, but I'd much rather cultivate joy! When the winter is cold and dark, I'm going to wrap up in a warm blanket, grab a hot latte, and cuddle by the fire.

Father, thank you for the multitude of blessings that you shower upon me each day. Forgive me for taking your gifts for granted. Open my eyes, to see your hand at work in my life, both on good days and hard days. Give me the resolve to cultivate joy even when it requires extra effort. Help me walk in joy so that I can likewise, walk in strength. I pray that my joy would be contagious and that it would inspire others to find a relationship with you. In Jesus name, Amen

Personal Reflection

First, prayerfully meditate on your emotional tendencies. Are there any seasons, months, days, or periods of time during which you struggle to walk in joy. Second, make a list of strategies that foster joy in your life. Begin to implement these strategies prior to any periods in which you tend to struggle. Even if you don't have an opportunity to emotionally prepare for a difficult season in advance, you can draw upon your strategies as soon as you need them.

Day 54

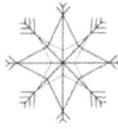

Day 55
Faithful Fertilizer

Yesterday, I mentioned that I struggle to maintain joy during the dark days of winter. Perhaps you enjoy the winter, but even so, we all face periods during which our hearts feel heavy. If we can persevere through hard seasons without giving up, however, God can use our struggles in powerful ways. Paul says, "We can rejoice, too, when we run into problems and trials, for we know that they help us develop endurance. And endurance develops strength of character, and character strengthens our confident hope of salvation. And this hope will not lead to disappointment. For we know how dearly God loves us," (Romans 5:3–5a). God isn't asking us to be happy about our trials or celebrate them, but he does call us to cultivate joy and hope in the midst of our struggles. Although the idea of maintaining joy throughout trials seems contrary to reason, our Father assures us that we won't be disappointed by our faith.

Trials are somewhat like the fertilizer that promotes the growth of beautiful flowers and nutritious foods. Considering the composition of fertilizer, the analogy is especially appropriate. The best fertilizers consist of decaying biomatter and animal waste. The nasty, stinky refuse provides nutrients essential for growth and fruitfulness. Although we don't want to smell, touch, or go near the smelly mess, we can look forward to the bounty it will produce. In a similar manner, we can appreciate our seasons of sadness and struggle.

To continue our less than appealing analogy, we can take steps to cultivate fecund fertilizer. I've learned from the disaster prepper fiction I enjoy reading that natural fertilizer, or compost, must have the right balance of nitrogen, carbon, air, and water. To achieve the best balance, the mixture needs green material, such as fruit and vegetable scraps, as well as brown material, such as dry leaves and coffee grounds. At the same time, certain substances should never be added. Meat scraps, fatty foods, dairy, and bone fragments can ruin your fertilizer. Similarly, waste from dogs and cats, which can carry parasites, should be kept away from the pile. As the compost "cooks," the mixture should stay damp, but not wet, and be stirred periodically.

You may have never wanted to know that much about compost, so allow me to connect the spiritual dots. When our life feels like a dark yucky mess, we can add nourishing elements that will promote healthy growth—prayer, Bible study, fellowship, and physical activity, for instance. Simultaneously, we should stay away from elements that will stymie future flourishing. Behaviors such as substance abuse, media overuse, and reclusiveness lead to self-destructive patterns that will ruin your potential for growth.

Just as compost requires months to transform into usable fertilizer, your season of perseverance and preparation may take time. As you wait, remember Romans 5. Your Father loves you dearly and you won't be disappointed by his love. When your season shifts and the spring arrives, your winter work will propel you into new growth!

Lord, thank you for your faithful love, in which I can place confident hope. Help me prepare for new growth as I endure through seasons of trial. Give me the wisdom to maintain healthy habits and teach me to incorporate new ones that will grow my capacity for perseverance. Protect me from temptation so that I don't foster habits that will hamper future growth. Refine my character and teach me to patiently trust in you. In Jesus' name, Amen

Personal Reflection

Make a list of your current trials, worries, and disappointments. Your struggle might be something as straightforward as my seasonal sadness or as complex as a broken marriage. Prayerfully consider how each item on your list can help you develop character in the present and foster growth in the future.

_____

_____

_____

_____

_____

_____

_____

_____

_____

_____

_____

_____

_____

Day 56
Poop Happens

One afternoon, Abel arrived home from school and received the worst surprise ever. As he walked from the car to the house, a bird pooped on his head. What are the odds of that happening? In the ten seconds between the car and the house, Abel was in precisely the right spot for the bird to fly over his head and poop at exactly the right time. I wouldn't have believed it if I hadn't seen it happen.

Abel's unfortunate incident illustrates the truth that bad things happen to good people. Sometimes, no rhyme or reason can explain a crappy circumstance. When these things happen, we often get angry with God or question his faithfulness. To blame God, however, comprehensively disregards the teaching of Scripture.

Jesus promises an abundant life (John 10:10), but nowhere in Scripture does he promise a life free of trials. In fact, we should be more surprised when good things happen. Jesus tells us, "In this world you will have trouble," (John 16:33) and John tells us that "the world around us is under the control of the evil one," (1 John 5:19b).

Thankfully, Jesus empowers and equips us to overcome our trials. John teaches that, "every child of God defeats this evil world, and we achieve this victory through our faith," (1 John 5:4). Even better, Jesus holds God's children securely within his protection so that "the evil one cannot touch them," (1 John 5:18b).

God's protection should be a source of great peace and confidence. We can hold fast to his promise when the enemy, though he can't touch us, can still throw poop in our direction. Next time he begins an assault, instead of getting angry at God, let's pick up our shield of faith. We can trust that our Father will provide exactly what we need at just the right time to give us victory over our adversary. As we discussed yesterday, God will take whatever stinky mess the enemy throws and transform it into fertilizer for healthy growth. Through the lens of faith, we can echo the words of Joseph in Genesis 50:20, "You intended to harm me, but God intended it all for good."

Lord, thank you for protecting me from the snares of the enemy. Thank you for turning his evil schemes into blessings. Forgive me for doubting you and failing to trust your goodness in seasons of struggle. Help me seize opportunities for victory rather than allowing anger or frustration to disrupt my trust in you. Grow my faith so that I see your hand of protection and provision in every situation. In Jesus' name, Amen.

Personal Reflection

As you encounter frustrating situations or persistent struggles today, remind yourself of the ways that God protects and provides for you in the present as well as the blessings that have resulted from past struggles.

_____

_____

_____

_____

_____

_____

Day 56

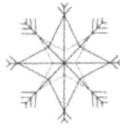

Day 57
In the Pit

The last couple of days we've talked about cultivating joy, faith, and perseverance in the face of trials. Today I would like to discuss the prophet Jeremiah, who embodied the idea of perseverance. You have probably heard of him as one of the major prophets in our Old Testament, but you may not know the details of his life. In addition to writing the book we call Jeremiah, he also wrote Lamentations, and is sometimes called "the weeping prophet," which should give you a clue as to the tenor of his life. Like many of us, he struggled to maintain joy in the midst of his trials, and for good reason.

God called Jeremiah to become a prophet at a young age, possibly as young as thirteen years old. He began his ministry during a time of idolatry and immorality in Judah. The young prophet implored his people to turn back to God and warned them of impending destruction. Despite his warnings, the other priests and prophets continued to preach that God was about to pour out his blessings upon Judah.

Because Jeremiah's message was contrary to what the people wanted to hear, they hated him. Even Jeremiah's closest friends denounced him (Jeremiah 20:10). He was beaten (18:18) and put in stocks (20:2). He was thrown into a cistern with no food or water and left to die (38:6). Although Jeremiah was rescued from the pit, any relief he might have felt would have been short-lived as he was forcibly sent into exile with the rest of his people (43:6). Jeremiah was so despised and despondent that he cried out to God, "I curse the day I was born! May no one celebrate the day of my birth. I curse the messenger who told my father, "Good news—you have a son!"'" (Jeremiah 20:14–15).

By worldly standards, Jeremiah's ministry was an abysmal failure. His message was rejected, he was personally despised, he felt like a failure, and he died without seeing his life bear fruit. Let me repeat that—Jeremiah went his entire lifetime without seeing the fruit of his prayer and his ministry. Nonetheless, he persevered:

> *O Lord, if you heal me, I will be truly healed;*
> *if you save me, I will be truly saved.*
> *My praises are for you alone!*
> *People scoff at me and say,*
> *"What is this 'message from the Lord' you talk*
> *about?*
> *Why don't your predictions come true?"*
> *Lord, I have not abandoned my job*
> *as a shepherd for your people.*
>
> ### Jeremiah 17:14–16a

Despite the physical suffering from being beaten, the emotional pain from being rejected, and the mental torment from knowing his people were about to be destroyed, Jeremiah never gave up!

We've probably never been thrown into a literal cistern like Jeremiah, but we sometimes feel as though our trials are trapping us inside a deep dark hole. Jeremiah shows us that overcoming struggles and persevering through trials can take longer than we expect or hope. His sad narrative reveals that we might never see the external or tangible fruit of our perseverance. However, I want to point out that although Jeremiah's life was a failure by worldly standards, his impact on the kingdom of God is immeasurable. His model of faith, obedience, and perseverance has inspired God's people for thousands of years.

Jeremiah doesn't just tell us, he shows us how to lean on God, even when the whole world feels like it's crashing down around us. And he points the way toward one who would persevere through even greater suffering—our Lord and Savior Jesus.

Heavenly Father, thank you for the example of Jeremiah. Help me learn from his example and be encouraged by his perseverance. I also thank you, Jesus, for likewise facing unimaginable trials on my behalf. Thank you for persevering through persecution and pain in order to conquer death and suffering for me. Help me to remember that you are my constant companion in the midst of every trial, and that you give me the ability to walk in freedom and hope, regardless of my circumstances. In moments of discouragement, when my struggles feel as though they have entrapped me, remind me by the power of your Spirit that you are near. As you help me navigate through trials with strength and character, I pray that you would allow my example of perseverance to inspire others. Give me opportunities to share the reason for my hope, which is you, my Savior, Jesus Christ. In your name, Amen.

Personal Reflection

Today we'll try something a little different. Re-read your list of struggles from two days ago, read the following visualization, and then close your eyes to slowly repeat the visualization in your mind. Imagine that you are trapped at the bottom of a dark pit, the walls of which are constructed by your struggles, worries, disappointments, and pain. You see no way out of the hole, but you sense that you aren't alone. Someone is in the pit with you—a man who has also faced many trials. In fact, he has suffered so greatly that he understands every trial you are going through. Because he persevered through his own unimaginable suffering, he was able to conquer each struggle on your behalf. As you gaze upon his face and listen to his voice, your companion reaches toward the wall of the dungeon and opens a door you hadn't noticed. He takes your hand and leads you from the darkness into an open landscape full of joy, freedom, and hope. He closes the door to your dark, cramped cell and you realize that this man, your Savior, has rescued you forever. You know will still face trials in the future, but you'll never again be trapped by them. Enjoying your freedom, you walk further from your pit in the light of the Lord. As your Savior walks by your side, you thank him for rescuing you and opening up a whole new world of possibilities.

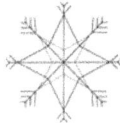

Day 58
Messy Mistakes

One afternoon, I noticed that Abel was by the front door with the toolbox. If you know Abel, you know that seeing him with the toolbox is cause for concern. He loves to take things apart and see how they work, but he doesn't always know how to reassemble them.

Per usual, I was torn between letting him learn and averting property damage. As a mother, I want to encourage his scientific curiosity, but as a homeowner, I want to keep my house in working order. So, with apprehension I questioned Abel about what he was planning. My kindhearted son explained that he was taking apart the doors and locks so that he could clean them up nicely for me. He assured me that he would be able to put everything back together.

Despite my misgivings, I allowed Abel to proceed. As often happens, however, Abel's good intentions outpaced his good sense. A short time later, he came to me and confessed that he was not, in fact, able to reassemble the doors and locks. I wasn't surprised since I knew that the probability of reassembly was low. I also wasn't worried because I knew that his father would be able to fix the problem.

I understand Abel's reckless curiosity, because he inherited it from me. I can't count the number of times my Heavenly Father has helped me clean up messes I've made. Time after time, my Lord has helped me reassemble things I've broken.

Yesterday, we discussed Jeremiah's ministry to Judah. The prophet begged his people to return to the Lord and repent of idolatry.

Nonetheless, they persisted in their spiral of sin and brought calamity upon themselves as God allowed Babylon to execute justice upon Judah. As their sins were wiped away, so was their homeland. In the midst of desolation, the Lord offered Jeremiah a message of hope, saying:

> *The time will come when I will heal Jerusalem's wounds and give it prosperity and true peace. I will restore the fortunes of Judah and Israel and rebuild their towns. I will cleanse them of their sins against me and forgive all their sins of rebellion. Then this city will bring me joy, glory, and honor before all the nations of the earth! The people of the world will see all the good I do for my people, and they will tremble with awe at the peace and prosperity I provide for them.*

Jeremiah 33:6–9

Through it all, God never abandoned his people. Despite their abominable sins and rejection of his love, the Father remained faithful to his children. Although God allowed them to face the consequences of their self-inflicted disaster, God was ready and waiting to heal their wounds, restore their peace, and bless their future.

Perhaps you've been hesitant to cry out to your Father because of your shame. Perhaps you are trying to reassemble the broken pieces of your life on your own. Perhaps you fear your Father and his response to your sin. Yet, our Father has revealed his character to us in Scripture. While he is a God of holiness and justice, he is also a God of love, mercy, and grace. Simply call out for his help and you'll truly see that "mercy triumphs over judgment," (James 2:13b).

Father, thank you for remaining faithful to me even when I am unfaithful. Thank you for forgiving my failures and helping me heal from every would, even those which are self-inflicted. I repent of avoiding you instead of running to you when I make messes. Help me learn from my mistakes so that I don't repeat them. Teach me to respond to the failures of others the way you respond to mine. Grow my capacity to not only forgive, but be an agent of healing in the lives of others. In Jesus' name, Amen.

Personal Reflection

Throughout your day, practice offering grace and kindness to anyone who annoys, offends, or hurts you. Each time you are tempted to become angry, remind yourself of God's forgiveness for your mistakes and thank him.

_____

_____

_____

_____

_____

_____

_____

_____

_____

_____

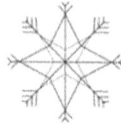

Day 59
Manual Labor

Yesterday we discussed our personal tendency to make messy mistakes and God's promise to forgive them. Although our Father is always faithful to provide grace and healing, he prefers that we avoid poor choices in the first place. God wants us cultivate a habit of seeking his guidance, making wise decisions, and staying out of trouble.

To help us remain on the right path, our Father has provided an instruction manual for life—the Bible. Trying to successfully navigate life without studying Scripture is as foolish as trying to assemble a piece of IKEA furniture without following the instructions. On the slim chance you are unfamiliar, IKEA is an international retailer of home furnishings. Their products are affordable, but only at the cost of your time, effort, and sanity. Each piece of furniture arrives in roughly a million pieces, with accompanying screws, bolts, and hinges. If you have any hope of successfully assembling your purchase, you must follow the instructions closely. Even with the manual, the furniture can be ridiculously hard to construct. I know from experience because we furnished our boys' playroom with IKEA furniture. The experience was not one I care to repeat.

I must confess that I'm not a manual reader. I enjoy figuring stuff out on my own and doing things my way. After making lots of mistakes and learning a few hard lessons, I'm finally learning that God's way is *always* better. Our lives are simply too valuable to ignore his instructions. Life is more fulfilling, peaceful, and joyful when we walk according to God's Word. According to Psalm 19,

> *The instructions of the Lord are perfect,*
> *reviving the soul.*
> *The decrees of the Lord are trustworthy,*
> *making wise the simple.*
> *The commandments of the Lord are right,*
> *bringing joy to the heart.*
> *The commands of the Lord are clear,*
> *giving insight for living.*
>
> ***Psalm 19:7–8***

Although Scripture is complex in many ways, the Word is simple enough for anyone to understand. Our Father empowers us with instructions that are trustworthy, right, and clear. Even better, since our Father's Word is perfect, we don't have to be!

Obviously, Scripture isn't as detailed as an IKEA manual. The Bible won't provide the solution to every question or the answer to every dilemma, but it will teach us to make wise decisions that honor God and bring us peace. We won't find a verse that tells us who to marry, but we will find passages that describe traits to look for in a spouse and how to have a healthy marriage. We won't find a verse to tell us which job to take, but we will find passages on discovering our purpose and discerning God's will. The more we study God's perfect manual, the better we'll understand how to make wise decisions and avoid the pitfalls of trying to figure out life on our own.

Lord, thank you for providing timeless wisdom so that I can live in joy and peace. Give me the discipline to study Scripture more faithfully. Enable me to see the blessing and benefit of spending time in your Word. Teach me to obey your instructions and make wise choices. I repent of going my own way and disregarding your teaching. Grow my desire to draw nearer to you through your Word. In Jesus' Name, Amen.

Personal Reflection

Prayerfully assess your attitude toward Scripture, read the following options, and select the one the best applies to you.

❋ Do you view the Bible as your manual for life and routinely seek guidance from its pages? If, so consider taking your study to the next level. For example, you might learn how to utilize a Bible software, memorize a new passage, or study a book with which you are unfamiliar.

❋ Do you value and trust God's Word, but lack consistency and obedience? If so, examine your routine and make space to spend time daily in God's Word. Make your study time non-negotiable, put it on your calendar, and continually remind yourself *why* the time is important. You aren't giving up your time, but rather gaining the blessings of joy and wisdom.

❋ Do you consider the Bible a book of interesting stories and ancient wisdom that is only marginally relevant for your life? I encourage you to watch the "Intro to the Bible" videos by the Bible Project. They just might help you see Scripture in a whole new light.

Scan the QR code for passages of Scripture

Day 60
The Raccoon Whisperer

Over the last couple of weeks, we've been working through a variety of heavy topics, such as sin, shame, and suffering. I would warrant a guess that you are more than ready to shift to some lighter fare. So, today I want to tell you about one of my favorite internet characters. You've probably heard of the "Dog Whisperer," but I'll bet you haven't heard of the "Racoon Whisperer." The Racoon Whisperer is a retired gentleman who lives in Canada. During the brutal, freezing winters, he feeds the wildlife around his rural home. In particular, he enjoys feeding the hoard of racoons who've learned they can find sustenance at his home.

The well-fed critters routinely gather at the gentleman's back door to wait for their dinner. When the Racoon Whisperer emerges, he sits upon a bench to provide grapes, hot dogs, carrots, dog food, and cookies. The animals crowd around, sit in his lap, and climb to his shoulders to eat food directly from his hands.

While I think racoons are absolutely adorable, I also know they can be pests. They'll get into your garbage and scatter the trash. They'll dig up your garden, eat your crops, and attack your pets. Even worse, they sometimes make nests in the roofs of houses, damaging shingles, insulation, and electrical wiring. Racoons can even carry and transmit a number of diseases that are communicable to humans. Although the animals have some positive behaviors, such as keeping their turf free from other pests, they are more foe than friend to humans.

The negative impact racoons can have on human living spaces is the reason the actions of the Racoon Whisperer are so surprising. He cares for a group of creatures that are typically shunned and avoided. In a similar manner, Paul instructs us to care for the less fortunate and to love the unlovely.

> *Since God chose you to be the holy people he loves, you must clothe yourselves with tenderhearted mercy, kindness, humility, gentleness, and patience. Make allowance for each other's faults, and forgive anyone who offends you. Remember, the Lord forgave you, so you must forgive others. Above all, clothe yourselves with love, which binds us all together in perfect harmony.*
>
> **Colossians 3:12–14**

Following the example of our Lord, we are called to extend grace and love. Throughout Scripture, God commands his people to care for orphans, widows, and the poor. During his earthly life, Jesus modeled compassion toward all people, including people society deemed unsavory.

Our Father desires that we love our friends, forgive our enemies, and show kindness to everyone. Perhaps God is calling you to respond to the annoying guy in your office with patience rather than annoyance. Maybe he is calling you to show compassion toward that weird family member you only see on holidays. Perhaps God wants you to listen to that "Debbie Downer" in your church and offer her words of encouragement. Perhaps he is leading you to minister to needy people in your community in tangible ways. Regardless of the specific situation, your kindness may be just as nourishing to those often shunned as hot dogs for racoons in sub-freezing weather.

Heavenly Father, thank you for showing compassion to me in moments when I require extra grace. Forgive me for shunning people in my life because they require extra compassion, patience, or emotional energy. Help me extend your love to people in my life who are less than desirable. Fill my heart with your love to such a degree that I no longer view other people as a burden or annoyance. Allow me to see your children through your eyes so that I appreciate their personhood and personality. In Jesus' name, Amen

Personal Reflection

Make a concerted effort to offer grace, forgiveness, and kindness to people you view as difficult today.

_____

_____

_____

_____

_____

_____

_____

_____

_____

_____

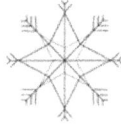

Day 61
Beautiful Buttercups

Daffodils are among my favorite flowers. Also known as buttercups or narcissus, the bright yellow and white flowers are among the first blooms each spring. Some years they start to emerge as early as December if we have several warm days in a row. In years past, I would panic if the first shoots appeared before the end of winter. Worried about the ruination of my beloved buttercups, I would cover them in glass bowls, mason jars, and plastic tablecloths to protect them from freezing when the temperature dropped.

While researching for devotional writing, I recently learned that my buttercups aren't likely to freeze even after they begin to sprout. Daffodils are tough, hardy perennials. They adapt quickly to temperature swings and can survive even freezing weather. The bulb of the flower is self-cloning, so not only is the plant robust, but it reproduces itself every year. The plants also contain oxalic acid, a poison that deters rodents, deer and other pests from snacking on them.

In other words, I don't have to worry about my daffodils blooming early. God has designed the bulbs to thrive despite unexpected and undesirable conditions. The Father causes them to bloom at just the right time.

God's timing works similarly in our lives. Despite our expectations, worries, and doubts, his timing is perfect. He is never late or early, and he has equipped us to thrive at just the right moment.

Abraham and Sarah struggled to trust God's timing. Sarah, in particular, doubted the Lord's promise of a son. As a woman well past child-bearing age, she found the idea laughable. Even a visit from three angels wasn't enough to convince her.

> *The Lord appeared again to Abraham near the oak grove belonging to Mamre. One day Abraham was sitting at the entrance to his tent during the hottest part of the day. He looked up and noticed three men standing nearby. When he saw them, he ran to meet them and welcomed them, bowing low to the ground. . . . "Where is Sarah, your wife?" the visitors asked. "She's inside the tent," Abraham replied. Then one of them said, "I will return to you about this time next year, and your wife, Sarah, will have a son!" Sarah was listening to this conversation from the tent. Abraham and Sarah were both very old by this time, and Sarah was long past the age of having children. So she laughed silently to herself and said, "How could a worn-out woman like me enjoy such pleasure, especially when my master—my husband—is also so old?" Then the Lord said to Abraham, "Why did Sarah laugh? Why did she say, 'Can an old woman like me have a baby?' Is anything too hard for the Lord? I will return about this time next year, and Sarah will have a son."*
>
> **Genesis 18:1–2, 9–14**

Just as God promised, Sarah soon bore a son. Her doubt and disbelief didn't derail God's plan or disrupt his timing. However, she could have saved herself substantial turmoil if she had simply trusted God.

Likewise, on a smaller scale, now that I've stopped worrying about my daffodils, I can enjoy them even more. Instead of fretting as the first shoots emerge and wasting time trying to protect them, I can watch them emerge with delight.

Let's trust God's timing and have faith in his behind-the-scenes work. He is preparing you to thrive at just the right time!

Lord, thank you for your perfect timing and sovereign guidance in my life. Help me have greater joy in the present moment instead of frustration over what might or might not happen in the future. Teach me to trust you even when your timing is different than my own. I repent of impatience, doubt, and mistrust. Grow me in patience, faith and fortitude as I wait upon your will. In Jesus' name, Amen.

Personal Reflection

Your reflection today is two-fold. First, list any situations in which you are hoping and praying God will soon move. Prayerfully entrust each to God and ask him to help you have greater faith as you wait upon his timing. Second, list any current circumstances for which you feel unprepared or inadequate. Prayerfully meditate on how God has already been preparing you for each and ask him to show you how you can partner with him to grow in proficiency or confidence.

_____

_____

_____

Day 61

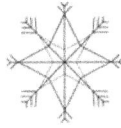

Day 62
Ghost Gardens

Yesterday we discussed my beautiful buttercups, which I recently learned are exceptionally hardy. The tough little bulbs are so resilient that they often outlive the gardener who planted them and the home beside which they were planted. In fact, the pattern in which the plants emerge can provide clues as to when the bulbs were planted. For example, planting flowers in squares and rectangles was popular in the 1700s, whereas bullseye patterns became popular in the antebellum period.[3]

These long-forgotten plots of daffodils are referred to as "ghost gardens." The designation may arise because daffodils are sometimes called "ghost flowers." I prefer, however, to imagine that the designation arose because those who planted the flowers are long gone. Although the original gardeners haven't tended their gardens for many years, their legacy continues to thrive.

When I first read about ghost gardens, I immediately thought about my own legacy. I pray that long after I am gone, the seeds I have planted will flourish. I hope that my loving labor will produce fruit that inspires others. I pray that my legacy will point people toward the beauty and grace of God.

---

[3] "Ghost Gardens of the South," The Forgotten South at https://the-forgottensouth.com/daffodil-history-ghost-gardens/.

The principle of legacy is found throughout Scripture. Abraham and Sarah, who we discussed yesterday, left a legacy that blessed generations because of their faithfulness to the Lord. Roughly 400 years after the Lord promised descendants, blessings, and land to Abraham, God brought the nation of Israel to the Promised Land. To commemorate the faithfulness of God, the people set-up a visible reminder of their legacy.

> *The people crossed the Jordan [into the Promised Land] on the tenth day of the first month. Then they camped at Gilgal, just east of Jericho. It was there at Gilgal that Joshua piled up the twelve stones taken from the Jordan River. Then Joshua said to the Israelites, "In the future your children will ask, 'What do these stones mean?' Then you can tell them, 'This is where the Israelites crossed the Jordan on dry ground.' For the Lord your God dried up the river right before your eyes, and he kept it dry until you were all across, just as he did at the Red Sea when he dried it up until we had all crossed over. He did this so all the nations of the earth might know that the Lord's hand is powerful, and so you might fear the Lord your God forever."*
>
> **Joshua 4:19–24**

Just as daffodils emerge each year and remind us of those who tended their gardens with care, Israel's monument told the story of God's faithfulness. The stones would remind future generations that the Lord is both powerful and true.

What type of legacy will you leave behind? Are you sowing seeds of faith, hope and love? Will the garden of your life produce a beautiful harvest and inspire generations to come? Planting and pruning aren't always easy, but your effort is worth it for the ones you love.

Lord, thank you for the generations of faithful men and women who have gone before me and left a legacy of faith. Thank you for the individuals who have poured inspiration and guidance into my life. Help me likewise be a source of encouragement to others. Forgive me for sometimes sowing seeds of bitterness or strife. Teach me how to sow seeds of faith, hope, and love that will produce beautiful fruit and nourish your kingdom.

Personal Reflection

First, prayerfully consider your own legacy. Whether or not you are cultivating a legacy with intentionality, you are sowing seeds. Second, take a few minutes to pray about the legacy you would like to leave behind. Third, write down a few ideas regarding how you can sow seeds with purpose and intentionality in order to leave the beautiful legacy God places upon your heart.

_____

_____

_____

_____

_____

_____

_____

_____

Day 62

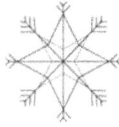

Day 63
Futile Flailing

If you recall, I love watching videos of wild animals. I also love watching clips of ordinary pets doing funny things. Recently, a friend of mine posted a video of her dog, Mister. The little terrier had received a treat and was diligently trying to bury the snack. He dug, pawed, and scratched at the tile kitchen floor, but his efforts were futile.

Mister's misguided endeavor fittingly illustrates our own futile flailings. We often desire a certain outcome, but our actions cannot and will not produce the desired result. Just as Mister wanted to bury his bone, no amount of digging on the tile was going to breach the surface of the floor.

In Scripture, the priests of Baal exemplified relentless futility. As the priests multiplied and spread across the country under the evil rulers Ahab and Jezebel, Elijah challenged them to a royal rumble. The prophet proposed a head-to-head match against the pagan priests that would decisively reveal whose God was more powerful. The conditions were simple. Both Elijah and the priests would sacrifice a burnt offering, but they were not allowed to light the fire. Only the gods could provide a fire to consume the sacrifice (1 Kings 18:18–24).

As the conflict began, the priests of Baal begged their god to light a fire. From morning until noon, they prayed to no avail. Becoming desperate, the priests began to dance, wail, and flail. When their writhing was unsuccessful, they began to cut their own flesh and yell even more loudly. Despite their intense effort, the priests' futile actions yielded absolutely zero results.

Isaiah's petition to the Lord was different in every way. As Isaiah approached the altar, he revealed just how powerful his God was. He didn't simply pray for God to light the fire. He poured water over the wood so that it would be virtually impossible to light by natural means. He knew his God held limitless power. He also knew the Lord was faithful. Isaiah's God didn't require flailing, dancing, wailing, or self-mutilation. Isaiah simply prayed and God lit the fire (1 Kings 18:24–38).

Hard work and maximum effort will not achieve desired outcomes if our goal is meaningless. No matter how much the prophets of Baal exerted themselves, no matter how hard Mister dug on the tile floor, they were not going to reach their objective. There's simply no power in futility, no matter how much we wish it or will it. The only true power is in our Lord. When we align ourselves with him, we have access to that power and strength. So instead of flailing through life with futility, let's step up to the altar of God and ask him to accomplish his good, perfect and powerful will through us.

Lord, thank you for working powerfully in my world and in me. Forgive me for trying to accomplish my own aims in my own strength. I repent of wasting precious moments on endeavors that are pointless and futile. Give me the clarity to seek after your will and the desire to accomplish your purposes. Help me forsake worthless pursuits and replace them with meaningful objectives. In Jesus' name, Amen.

Personal Reflection

First, write down several short-term goals and several long-term goals. Prayerfully evaluate each one and allow the Lord to shift or replace any objectives that might be misaligned. Second, ask God to show you how you can replace any futile strategies with meaningful steps toward accomplishing worthwhile goals.

_____

_____

_____

_____

_____

_____

_____

_____

_____

_____

_____

_____

_____

_____

_____

_____

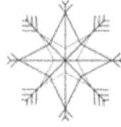

Day 64
Communication Breakdown

Yesterday we discussed our tendency to engage in futile pursuits. We often desire a certain outcome, but our actions cannot and will not produce the desired result. Like the dog trying to bury his bone on a tile floor or the priests of Baal trying to compel their non-existent God to action, meaningless efforts produce lackluster results.

In a similar manner, our words often produce undesirable outcomes. When we speak in anger, foolishness, or pride, our words actually become counterproductive. If our objective is to end an argument by making an irrefutable point and decimating our companion, we'll actually provoke greater conflict. According to Proverbs 15:1, "A gentle answer deflects anger, but harsh words make tempers flare." Alternatively, perhaps you want to astound associates and impress colleagues with your knowledge. Your prideful words will actually make you sound like a fool. Proverbs 15:2 continues, "The tongue of the wise makes knowledge appealing, but the mouth of a fool belches out foolishness."

Whatever our objective, the authors of Scripture advocate two wise communication strategies. First, we should master the skill of keeping our mouths shut. According to Proverbs 13:3, "Those who control their tongue will have a long life; opening your mouth can ruin everything." Second, we should only speak words that encourage others, foster peace, and spread kindness. In addition to cooling hot tempers, gentle words nourish the spirit (Proverbs 15:4), avert sin, foster wisdom, and accomplish great feats (Proverbs 10:18– 21). In short, we can summarize the teaching of Scripture with a familiar aphorism, "If you don't have anything nice to say, don't say anything at all."

Lord, thank you for giving me the faculty to communicate wisely. I repent for the times when I've spoken in anger, foolishness, or pride. Teach me to hold my tongue and listen more than I speak. Give me the self-discipline to refrain from speaking angry or hurtful words. Help me grow in Christ's likeness so that I no longer desire to speak words that would harm others. Make me aware of opportunities to bring peace and encourage others with life-giving words. Empower me to speak in ways that accomplish much for your kingdom. In Jesus' name, Amen.

Personal Reflection

Strive for productive communication today. Instead of simply trying to say nice things or offer disingenuous compliments, focus on the desired outcome of each interaction. Can you foster peace, spiritual growth, professional development, relational health, honest communication, faithful service, or sacrificial love? Offer as many wise words as you can fit into the day because tomorrow you are going to practice keeping your mouth shut!

_____

_____

_____

_____

_____

_____

Day 64

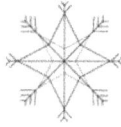

Day 65
Complex Communication

Yesterday, we discussed strategies for productive communication. In general, the authors of Scripture advocate two approaches: speaking words that edify or keeping our mouths shut. Today and tomorrow, we'll continue talking about communication, but with methods that extend beyond words.

To illustrate, I'd like to tell you about the complex communication strategies of wolves. Obviously, wolves can't talk, but they do have a variety of communication methods at their disposal. Wolves can transmit information through vocalizations such as yelping, whining, howling, or growling. Most communication, though, is conducted through body language, facial expression, and scent.

Wolves use non-vocal communication to signal pack status, emotional state, territorial range, and social intent. Pack dominance is signified by an erect posture and lifted tail, while submission is expressed by rolling over and exposing the belly. The lowest members of the pack signal subordination by maintaining a crouched posture and tucked tail in the presence of other wolves. Packmates also express their desire to play through cues such as bowing and hopping. Affection can be conveyed through licking, pawing, and even play-fighting.

We'll talk more about wolf communication methods tomorrow, but let me pause to make a point. Wolves aren't hampered by their inability to speak. Their non-verbal communication might even be more truthful and coherent than human conversation at times.

Perhaps human interactions would be more productive if we learned to communicate honestly and intelligently, without the option to utilize manipulative, deceptive, or destructive words. The Psalmist likewise understood the wisdom of verbal restraint. He prays, "Set a guard over my mouth, Lord; keep watch over the door of my lips," (Psalm 141:3).

The discipline of silence is not intrinsically beneficial, yet practicing quietude trains us to think before speaking and choose our words wisely. Furthermore, holding our tongues enables us to hear others more clearly and more readily perceive God's voice.

When I was a young believer in Christ, silence became a refuge that sheltered me from embarrassment and regret. Having spouted countless shameful, foolish, and hurtful words, I had no desire to continue placing my foot in my mouth. So, my encouragement to you is that God can transform your own spigot of shameful words into a fountain of life and joy. I know from personal experience!

Lord, thank you for giving me the faculty to communicate wisely. Forgive me for spewing angry, foolish, and hurtful words. Teach me to hold my tongue, cultivate a discipline of silence, and listen more than I speak. As I quiet my own words, help me hear your voice more clearly. Teach me to think before I speak and choose my words wisely. I pray that my speech would be a source of life and joy to those around me. In Jesus' name, Amen.

Personal Reflection

As promised, you are going to practice the discipline of silence today. You don't have to refrain from speaking all day long. Rather, you'll remain quiet whenever possible and pause to think before you speak. You'll communicate concisely and avoid idle chatter. You'll listen and learn instead of offering your own opinions. From your place of silence, seek to better understand those around you and discern the will of God.

Day 66
More than Words

Today, we'll continue our discussion of communication. As I explained yesterday, wolves utilize remarkably complex methods of communication that are rooted in their physiology. Although the canines sometimes utilize vocalization, most information is conveyed through body language, facial expression, and scent.

A powerful sense of smell enables wolves to procure a wealth of information. From the scent of urine alone, wolves identify peers, determine gender, and evaluate potential mates. A paired couple can even broadcast their relationship status by scent marking together.

Wolves also utilize their sense of smell to locate unusual or strong odors, such as decaying carcasses. Once found, the wolves roll in the source of the stink, coating their fur in the smelly perfume. Researchers are uncertain why wolves and other species of canines "scent roll," but some experts theorize that the foreign odors help wolves mask their scent in order to approach prey undetected.

The most fascinating avenue of wolf communication is, in my opinion, facial expression, which conveys a dynamic range of emotional and social information. For instance, bared teeth and curled lips are clear signals of anger and aggression. Lowered ears, wide eyes, and raised eyebrows convey fear. Loose lips and a relaxed jaw signal friendliness. A tilted head and pricked ears suggest curiosity.

Equally fascinating, physical signals account for more than 50% of human communication. Thus, if we want our communication to be healthy and productive, understanding body language is essential. Accurately interpreting unspoken information equips us to respond with sensitivity, and managing our own non-verbal signals helps build trust and facilitate understanding.

Giving attention to unspoken signals helps us better understand what our peers are trying to communicate. Equipped with greater awareness and insight, we can more successfully resolve conflict and facilitate satisfying interactions. According to Proverbs 18:20, "Wise words satisfy like a good meal; the right words bring satisfaction." The verse refers to the satisfaction produced by wise words, but I believe that the principle applies to other forms of communication as well.

Although I can't say for certain whether wolves feel satisfaction, their straightforward signals result in safety, sustenance, and stability. Using non-verbal communication, packmates help one another procure food and defend the pack, while individual wolves foster relational bonds, choose mates, and show affection. Judging by their playful antics, affectionate gestures, and protective behaviors, pack life certainly appears to be satisfying. Let's learn a lesson from the wolves and start to listen with more than our ears.

Father, thank you for creating me with the capacity to communicate with sophistication. Help me to bear your image well by speaking words that are wise and edifying. I repent of gossip, slander, and other hurtful words I've spoken. Teach me to hold my tongue so that I never speak unkindly or foolishly. Give me greater discernment in order to understand the non-verbal signals of others and manage my own. Grow my communicative abilities so that my interactions produce joy and satisfaction. In Jesus' name, Amen.

Day 66

Personal Reflection

Continue practicing the discipline of silence today. As you listen to the spoken words of others, also cultivate a habit of paying attention to body language and non-verbal cues. Consider how the additional information can help you dialogue more productively and respond more thoughtfully.

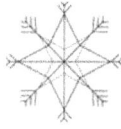

Day 67
Mixed Signals

The last few days, we've been exploring strategies for fostering communication that is wise, productive, and satisfying. As we've discussed, wolves utilize remarkably complex methods of communication, which include vocalization, body language, facial expression, and scent. Human communication, likewise, utilizes both verbal and non-verbal signals. Yet because we rely so heavily on speech, we often neglect the other communicative tools at our disposal.

Unlike wolves, humans have the capacity to transmit conflicting messages simultaneously. We may express one sentiment via speech, but send a wholly different message with our body. For example, we might say, "I'm fine," while our body communicates "I'm furious." Standing with rigid posture, crossed arms, and narrowed eyes sends a resounding message of anger that blatantly conflicts with our conciliatory words.

Transmitting mixed signals yields interactions that can be annoying, embarrassing, or even offensive. However, sending conscientious cues fosters healthy rapport. For example, a subtle smile, a tilted head, and slightly raised eyebrows convey interest and build trust, while a downcast head and averted eyes give the impression of boredom or dishonesty. Along similar lines, a confident posture and good eye contact communicate engagement and trustworthiness, while fidgeting and looking around communicates distraction and anxiety.

By learning to utilize both verbal and non-verbal signals, we promote cohesive conversation. In fact, learning to communicate with clarity is vital for the health of the soul and body. According to Proverbs, "The heart of the wise instructs his mouth; and with his lips he continually promotes understanding. Pleasant words are like honey from the honeycomb, sweet to the soul and healthy for the bones," (Proverbs 16:23–24, my translation). These verses remind us that wise communication is intentional, clear, and beneficial.

Long before any words are spoken, we should think about what we want to communicate and how we can convey that information in a way that promotes understanding. In doing so, our conversations not only become more productive, but we bless our loved ones with happiness and health.

Father, thank you for allowing me to promote fulfillment and understanding through communication. I repent of being careless with my words, actions, and unspoken signals. Teach me to use all of the tools you've provided in order to communicate wisely. Help me learn to be more intentional and thoughtful about the messages I send with my verbal and non-verbal signals. Grow my self-control so that I am never tempted to send messages that hurt or mislead others. Give me the discernment to communicate in ways that make my relationships healthier. In Jesus' Name, Amen

Personal Reflection

Continue honing the skills we've discussed over the last few days. Listen more and speak less. Give attention to both verbal and non-verbal cues. Consider how the additional information can help you dialogue more productively and respond more thoughtfully. Think before speaking and consider how you can use your words and body language to foster clear communication.

_____

_____

_____

_____

_____

_____

_____

_____

_____

_____

_____

_____

_____

_____

_____

_____

Day 68
How Do I Love Thee?

I was fascinated recently to learn that many animals and insects possess rudimentary counting skills. Wolves use math to determine how many members of the pack are needed to hunt different types of prey. Bears, whose cognitive abilities have gone largely unresearched, have demonstrated the ability to utilize basic math skills to forage for food more effectively.[4]

As humans with the capacity for higher thinking, we are capable of complex mathematical reasoning and often count without even realizing it. In "Sonnet 43" published in 1850, Elizabeth Barrett Browning asked, "How do I love thee? Let me count the ways." Sadly, we often number our offenses more readily than our affections. We store each transgression, insult, and inadequacy in the arsenal of our memory, waiting to take it out and throw it like a grenade when we want to gain the upper hand.

Stockpiling offenses, however, is the opposite of showing love. Peter explains that "love covers a multitude of sins," (1 Peter 4:8), and Paul teaches that "[love] keeps no record of being wronged," (1 Corinthians 13:4–7). Paul also informs us that Jesus models the way he

---

[4] "Black Bears Can "Count" as Well as Primates," National Geographic at https://www.nationalgeographic.com/animals/article/120829-black-bears-cognition-animals-science.

calls us to love others. According to 2 Corinthians 5:19, "In Christ, God was reconciling the world to himself, not counting their offenses against them," (my translation).

Just as we should refuse to keep a count of wrongs perpetrated against us, we should likewise refrain from keeping a list of our good deeds. If we give for the purpose of getting something in return, we haven't truly shown love. In fact, keeping a record of our gifts, kind words, and acts of service so that we can later cash them in is manipulative behavior. Instead, our Lord models selfless love and generous affection. He delights to give us the desires of our hearts (Psalm 20:4), abundant grace (Ephesians 4:7), and eternal life (John 3:16). Even better, he gives freely and requires nothing in return (Romans 8:32).

So, despite Browning's poetic words, love is not a matter of counting. Our Father's love is infinite, and as his children, we have access to his immeasurable affection. As we increasingly become saturated in his love, counting the mistakes of others becomes unappealing and our own good deeds become less worthy of mention. Perhaps we should rephrase the classic expression and say, "How do I love thee? Let me *not* count the ways."

Lord, thank you for not numbering my sins or holding them against me. Forgive me for keeping a record of offenses and a list of good deeds. Free me from the bondage of needing vengeance for my hurts and rewards for my kindness. Teach me to love selflessly, forgive unconditionally, and give generously. In Jesus' Name, Amen.

Personal Reflection

Practice showing love that is selfless and generous today. At every opportunity, forgive offense and offer kindness, expecting nothing in return.

Day 68

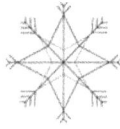

Day 69
Love, Patience, and Pumpkins

I'm delighted by fall gourds and pumpkins. I love looking at the variety of different shapes and color combinations. Last fall, after spending a ridiculously long time looking over my options, I chose four large gourds to display on my front porch.

As Christmas approached, all my pumpkins were still robust and healthy. I couldn't bear throwing them away, so I moved them to the back porch. My intention was to cut them open and save the seeds so that I could plant my own colorful gourds and pumpkins during the next growing season.

Weeks turned into months, and my gourds started to deflate. My boys asked when I was going to throw them away, but I still hoped to find time to harvest the seeds. Eventually, I admitted to myself and everyone else that I wasn't going to harvest the pumpkin seeds.

Shortly thereafter, I noticed my husband, Wesley, on the back porch with gloves and a trash bag. Without a word, he had decided to clean up my mess. I rushed outside nervously expecting to find a very irritated husband. Our interaction went something like this:

Andrea: "I'm so sorry. I promise I'll clean the mess."
Wesley: "No problem. Do you still want some seeds?"
Andrea: "Well . . . yes, that would be nice." [gets spoon to scoop out seeds]
Wesley: [sits down to wait]

Andrea: "What are you doing?"

Wesley: "Have you got all the seeds you want? If so, I'll finish cleaning up."

Andrea: "You seriously don't have to clean up this mess."

Wesley: "I don't mind. I know you're really busy."

Andrea: [gets pumpkin seeds and goes inside]

Wesley: [cleans up goopy, slimy pumpkin mess]

Why did Wesley insist on cleaning up my mess? I'm absolutely certain that he didn't enjoy the scent and texture of rotten pumpkins. I'm also certain he could have found a more enjoyable way to spend his time.

Wesley is kind to me because he loves me and he loves God. He models Paul's description of love in 1 Corinthians 13.

> *Love is patient and kind. Love is not jealous or boastful or proud or rude. It does not demand its own way. It is not irritable, and it keeps no record of being wronged. It does not rejoice about injustice but rejoices whenever the truth wins out. Love never gives up, never loses faith, is always hopeful, and endures through every circumstance.*

1 Corinthians 13:4–7

During our more than 20 years of marriage, Wesley has tolerated much worse from me than rotten pumpkins. I routinely make messes, say inappropriate things, and do things that would challenge the patience of a saint. Just as routinely, Wesley is kind, faithful, and forgiving.

I recognize how insanely blessed I am to have someone who loves me faithfully. But the truth is that we all have someone who loves us just as extravagantly. Jesus is always kind, he is always faithful, and he is always patient. He forgives our failures and celebrates our wins. Jesus doesn't get angry when we make a mess; he helps us clean it up! I want you to know that you are richly loved by your savior.

You may have never experienced selfless love from another human. You may have been disappointed by people you love. You may have even been betrayed, rejected, and abandoned. The truth is that every person in your life will fall short of the love of Christ. Even Wesley messes up from time to time. But we have a Savior who will never fail and who will always stay by our side.

Lord, thank you for loving me faithfully and extravagantly. Help me to grasp the depth and breadth of your love. Help me to see your love clearly, rather than filtering your love through the disappointments I have experienced. Help me to live in the light of your kindness, patience, and forgiveness. Give me opportunities to show your love to others so that they can experience your grace. In Jesus, name, Amen.

Personal Reflection

Re-read 1 Corinthians 13:4–7 above and replace "love" with "Jesus" (i.e., Jesus is patient and kind . . .), and thank your Savior for his unconditional love. Then read the passage once more and replace "love" with your own name. Confess the words over yourself and seek opportunities to reflect the love of Jesus today.

_____

_____

_____

_____

_____

Day 69

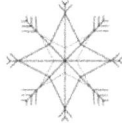

Day 70
Great Expectations

Yesterday I told you about Wesley patiently cleaning up my rotten pumpkins. As soon as I realized he was cleaning up my mess, I became worried. I was certain he was angry with me and that he was only cleaning the rotten pumpkins out of frustration with my procrastination. Yet, when I nervously offered to take over the clean-up, Wesley was anything but angry. He legitimately wanted to help.

Why do we so often assume the worst when people give their best? Granted, our negative assumptions are sometimes based on established patterns and past evidence. However, just as Christ offers grace to you and I, we should offer grace to others. Rather than assuming ill intent, nefarious motives, or deceptive designs, our hearts should be so filled with Christ's love that we see the best in every word and deed.

When we expect the worst or assign false motives to others, we judge their character, even if only in our own mind. Yet, Christ instructs us not to judge or condemn others. He teaches,

> *Do not judge others, and you will not be judged. Do not condemn others, or it will all come back against you. Forgive others, and you will be forgiven. Give, and you will receive. Your gift will return to you in full—pressed down, shaken together to make room for more,*

running over, and poured into your lap. The amount
you give will determine the amount you get back.
Luke 6:37–38

Based on the words of Jesus, we can conclude that if we give grace and kindness, we'll be blessed in return. We might not always receive material blessings or verbal accolades, but we'll reap abundant relational health and spiritual growth.

Assigning ill intent should cause us to examine our own heart more so than the motives of others. We tend to project onto others the way we would behave in a certain situation. For example, had anyone in my family left a stinking pile of rotten pumpkins on my patio, I would have been furious. Similarly, in 1 John 3:12, John teaches that Cain murdered his own brother, Abel, because of the hate in his own heart, not because of Abel's actions. When we assume ill intent or assign malice to the actions of others, we create relational friction and strife, sometimes from thin air, sometimes from our own hearts.

We'll discuss the topic further tomorrow. For today, simply foster grace. Pour out the best your heart has to offer, and expect every interaction to be a blessing. Remember that as you give trust you make room for even greater blessings to pour out and overflow in your life.

Lord, thank you for seeing something in me worthy of saving. Thank you for selflessly giving of yourself and forgiving me even when I was your enemy. Help me to likewise see the good in others and forgive their shortcomings. Forgive me for judging others harshly and expecting the worst of them. Teach me to see people from your perspective and to encourage them to become their best self. Make me a blessing to others and give me the strength to love every person no matter how they respond to my kindness and grace. In Jesus' name, Amen

Personal Reflection

Be mindful of your interpersonal interactions today. Make a conscious decision to extend grace and trust. Instead of assuming the worst, ask questions and extend kindness. If relational friction arises, examine your heart to see if you are contributing to the strife. Regardless of the source, seek to offer encouragement rather than condemnation.

_____

_____

_____

_____

_____

_____

_____

_____

_____

_____

_____

_____

_____

Day 71

Expect the Best — Prepare for the Worst

Yesterday we discussed extending grace and kindness to the people with whom we interact. When we extend grace, we increase the likelihood of receiving blessings in return. However, the life, ministry, and death of Jesus teaches us that kindness won't always be reciprocated. This is why we must also cultivate wisdom and forgiveness. Paul teaches us to expect other people to have flaws and make allowance for them.

> *Since God chose you to be the holy people he loves, you must clothe yourselves with tenderhearted mercy, kindness, humility, gentleness, and patience. Make allowance for each other's faults, and forgive anyone who offends you. Remember, the Lord forgave you, so you must forgive others. Above all, clothe yourselves with love, which binds us all together in perfect harmony. And let the peace that comes from Christ rule in your hearts. For as members of one body you are called to live in peace. And always be thankful. Let the message about Christ, in all its richness, fill your lives. Teach and counsel each other with all the wisdom he gives.* **Colossians 3:12–16**

We can "make allowance for each other's faults" by taking a few advance measures. Let me illustrate the principle using my schnauzers, whom I love fiercely. They bring so much joy to my life that I am willing to forgive any infraction on their part. I acknowledge they are likely to track mud into my house and onto my bed, that they sometimes dig into the kitchen trash, that they bark loudly in inconvenient moments, and that occasionally dig holes in my beautiful yard.

Because I care for them deeply, I've taken several steps to make allowance for their faults. First, I acknowledge that they are dogs. In other words, I set realistic expectations for their behavior. Second, I forgive them in advance. Because I've set realistic expectations, I know they are going to misbehave at times. Third, I take preventative action to mediate damage. For example, I wipe off their feet when they enter the house and I don't put tempting snacks in accessible trash cans. Fourth and finally, I try to teach them better behaviors and healthier ways to express their instincts.

Similar strategies will benefit our human relationships as well. We can set realistic expectations and decide to forgive in advance. We can put safeguards in place to mediate the fallout of mistakes. Then, once we've fostered an atmosphere of grace and love, we'll have the relational equity for productive dialogue, wise counsel, and spiritual growth.

When love and peace are the ruling principle of our lives, grace and forgiveness are a natural response to the failures of others. Further, as Paul reminds us, we often need forgiveness ourselves. Let's love well, foster forgiveness, expect the best, and prepare for the worst.

Lord, thank you for forgiving me even though I don't deserve your grace. Thank you for loving me even when I am unlovely. Help me to extend the same forgiveness, grace, and love to other people. Give me the fortitude to forgive every offense. Help me to assess every situation with wisdom and discernment, then take proactive measures to ensure harmony and peace. Teach me to foster relational health and equip me to provide wise counsel.

Deepen my relationship with you so that love and peace are my guiding principles in every interaction. In Jesus' name, Amen.

Personal Reflection

Continue to be mindful of your interpersonal interactions today. Consider how you can proactively prepare for interactions that might arise. Seek to offer compassion rather than condemnation when appropriate.

_____

_____

_____

_____

_____

_____

_____

_____

_____

_____

_____

_____

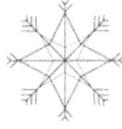

Day 72
Contentious Conversation

The last few days, we've talked about how to foster interactions that honor Jesus and encourage others. Offering kindness, however, can become difficult in moments of tension, anger, or disagreement. During such interactions, our emotions can override the rational part of our brain and cause us to view our peers as enemies. For instance, when I finished my PhD, I decided that my graduation gift should be more dogs. Wesley wouldn't even consider adding to our schnauzer pack, and I was furious. For days, I felt underappreciated and unloved. Instead of listening to Wesley's rational arguments—more vet bills, chewed up furniture, accidents in the house—I viewed him as an adversary to be conquered. Eventually, I accepted defeat, acknowledging that Wesley's arguments were valid. However, I could have avoided much marital strife if I had kept my emotions in check.

Preventing emotional override requires a great deal of mental strength and spiritual maturity. With practice, however, we can prevent such temporary enmity before it leads to permanent relational fractures. Although we may disagree, sometimes vehemently, we must maintain love, kindness, and respect as we interact with each other. Paul reminds us not to "use foul or abusive language. Let everything you say be good and helpful, so that your words will be an encouragement to those who hear them. Get rid of all bitterness, rage, anger, harsh words, and slander, as well as all types of evil behavior. Instead, be kind to each other, tenderhearted, forgiving one another, just as

God through Christ has forgiven you," (Ephesians 4:29, 31–21). Even when we feel angry, we should never speak words with the intention to harm, get revenge, or gain the upper hand.

We shouldn't want to "win" an argument because, in doing so, someone has to "lose." Instead, the goal of an argument should be to find a solution, reach an understanding, achieve a compromise, or even agree to disagree. We must remember that we are communicating with someone we care for, not trying to defeat an opponent.

Relationships are more important than being right. Sharing the love of Christ is more important than winning an argument. Instead of engaging in interactions with the goal of getting our way, we should seek mutual understanding and healthy dialogue. Through Christ's love, we can remain loyal allies, not hostile foes.

Lord, thank you for loving me even when I was your enemy. Thank you for teaching me a better way—how to love my all people and extend grace to those who've made mistakes. Help me remain calm during heated interactions and remember that other people are never my enemy. Give me a desire to encourage my peers rather than bolstering my own pride. Help me become humbler as I seek to build healthy relationships and edify others. Teach me to respond wisely instead of reacting rashly in emotional moments. Forgive me for times when I've lost my temper and hurt or belittled others. Help me learn from my mistakes so that I can more effectively share your love. In Jesus' name, Amen.

Personal Reflection

Prayerfully meditate on your personal tendencies in heated interactions. Do you allow emotions to override the rational part of your mind? Do you say hurtful words and react rashly? Be mindful of your interactions today, giving special attention to your words and behaviors in tense moments. Be intentional about promoting

understanding and relational health rather than seeking to win arguments and get your own way.

_____

_____

_____

_____

_____

_____

_____

_____

_____

_____

_____

_____

_____

Day 73

When Bears Attack

I've never been attacked by a bear, and I hope you haven't either. I do know that being prepared and informed, as we discussed yesterday, helps us stay safe in that unlikely eventuality. Learning about a few basic behaviors and strategies can, therefore, decrease the likelihood of an encounter turning into an attack.

If we see a bear, according to the National Park Service, we should speak softly and stand calmly in one place. We should also raise our arms in the air to appear larger and more intimidating. We should never run away or scream, which will cause bears to perceive us as prey and incite their aggression.[5]

Most often though, bears prefer to avoid a confrontation with humans. The imposing creatures will stand tall when they see people, but their posture isn't for the purpose of intimidation. Usually, they simply want to get a better look at the unexpected visitors. Their priority is making sure their food, cubs, and territory are safe.

Understanding bear encounters can also provide insight into humans. We sometimes approach interpersonal interactions as warily as a bear attack. We might be quiet and guarded or puff up to seem

---

[5] This devotional is not a definitive guide to bear encounter safety. For more information, see "Staying Safe Around Bears," National Park Service at https://www.nps.gov/subjects/bears/safety.htm.

more imposing. Alternatively, we might misread the intentions of our peers, interpreting their curiosity as aggression or their friendliness as a threat.

Instead of posturing and posing, however, we are called to interact with authenticity and honesty. Paul exhorts, "Don't just pretend to love others. Really love them. Hate what is wrong. Hold tightly to what is good. Love each other with genuine affection, and take delight in honoring each other," (Romans 12:9–10).

We know that authentic encounters and genuine affection lead to healthy relationships and meaningful connections. Yet, we often hesitate because authenticity places us in a vulnerable position. Perhaps you've tried to foster authentic relationships in the past. You've cared for others, bared your soul, trusted someone with your heart, and been betrayed, deceived, manipulated, or rejected.

When we open our hearts to others, we leave them exposed to potential harm. At the same time, however, keeping ourselves closed off to authentic relationships poses an even greater danger. We might protect ourselves from emotional harm, but we also cordon ourselves off from love, growth, fulfillment, and joy. As the modern proverb says, "no risk, no reward"!

Lord, thank you for placing people around me who enrich my life. Help me to love them with authenticity and honor them with joy. Give me the wisdom to discern who I can trust with my innermost thoughts, hopes, dreams, and struggles. Give me the courage to follow your guidance and trust companions you place in my path. Show me how to be a good friend so that others can likewise place their trust in me. As I foster healthy relationships, give me opportunities to lead others toward a closer relationship with you. In Jesus' name, Amen

Personal Reflection

As you interact with other people today, strive to be authentic.
Show genuine kindness even in situations you find threatening. Be
sincere rather than posturing to make yourself look bigger and better
than others.

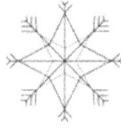

Day 74
Biting the Hands that Feeds

Yesterday we talked about fostering authenticity in our relationships. Though puffing up and posturing is an excellent strategy for bear encounters, it's a horrible strategy for connecting with fellow humans. Healthy interactions begin with authenticity and honesty. We must take risks and make ourselves vulnerable if we hope to develop meaningful relationships.

But what happens when we open our hearts and our hands, then get hurt? What happens when we get close to someone, serve them with love, and our kindness is met with betrayal?[6] I recall feeling used and hurt during one season of ministry. I felt as though I was on the receiving end of the phrase "don't bite the hand that feeds." I had reached out a helping hand and gotten bitten. In return for my service and love, I was rewarded with animosity and antagonism. As I processed my emotions and attempted to forgive the offense, Jesus reminded me that he was likewise reviled by those he came to serve. Peter explains, "[Jesus] did not retaliate when he was insulted, nor threaten revenge when he suffered. He left his case in the hands of God, who always judges fairly," (1 Peter 2:23).

---

[6] By rejection and betrayal, I am not referring to abuse, which is a different matter that calls for an altogether different response.

Jesus suffered betrayal more profound than we can imagine. A member of his innermost circle of friends betrayed him to the authorities. The very people he came to serve crucified him. He was mocked, spit upon, flogged, and violently murdered (Matthew 20:19). Through it all, he refused to retaliate. His love was so great that he was willing to endure unimaginable suffering in order to help the people he loved.

As I meditated upon the sacrifice of Christ, my own offense began to pale in comparison. My hurting heart slowly began to heal as I reflected upon the honor of following in the footsteps of my Savior. My desire to retaliate transformed into compassion and empathy.

If we foster close connections, we'll almost certainly get hurt at some point. We can decide to retaliate or seize the opportunity to walk in greater intimacy with our Savior. Like Jesus, we can entrust our Father to judge justly. I don't know about you, but I'm relieved to leave justice in his hands.

Lord, thank you for modeling authentic love and friendship. Teach me to offer compassion instead of retaliation. Forgive me for holding offense in my heart and help me learn to readily forgive. Fill my heart with love so great that I'm not afraid to foster close relationships. Show me how to serve others with selfless love and wisdom. In Jesus' name, Amen.

Personal Reflection

Have you been hurt or betrayed by someone close to you? How did you respond? What can you learn from your experience so that you'll be better prepared in the future? How can you respond to the one(s) who hurt you with greater maturity? How can you continue to foster healthy relationships while minimizing the potential for harm?

Day 75
Wounds of a Friend

Over the last week, we've been discussing strategies for healthy relationships and meaningful interactions. Sadly though, our efforts to show genuine affection and offer kindness aren't always reciprocated. Sometimes we open our hearts and give love only to face profound betrayal. Sometimes we pray for guidance and follow God's direction only to be faced with overwhelming disappointment.

King David lamented such rejection in his own life. In Psalm 55:12–14, he cries out to the Lord, "It is not an enemy who taunts me—I could bear that. It is not my foes who so arrogantly insult me—I could have hidden from them. Instead, it is you—my equal, my companion and close friend. What good fellowship we once enjoyed as we walked together to the house of God." I would guess that we can all empathize with David as he recalled happier times with a dear friend. Everyone has experienced the wounds of a friend at some point in life.

Some wounds are so deep that they cause us to question our faith and doubt the goodness of our Father. Yet, God is not the one who failed us. As humans, we have free will, and we all make bad choices. Sometimes, sadly, we are on the receiving end of horrible decisions. Through his own experience of betrayal, David models a godly response and encourages us to follow his example. David declares, "I will call on God, and the Lord will rescue me," (Psalm 55:16). A few verses later, he exhorts, "Give your burdens to the Lord, and he will take care of you. He will not permit the godly to slip and fall," (Psalm 55:22).

In addition to David's righteous response to betrayal, I would like to share the testimony of a dear friend who fervently held to her faith during a season of life-changing disappointment. My friend, Amy, remained single into her 30s, waiting on God to reveal her future husband. At 32, she finally met the right man, sensed God's blessing, and got married. As for what followed, I'll let Amy share the rest in her own words.

> We worshiped together and dreamed big dreams of a family and a God first life. Yet, over the course of our new life together, old demons in my husband's life started to recapture ground. Drugs became what he wanted instead of following God or being a husband. I fervently prayed for him and continued to attend church without him. I still believed God was working in both of us and that our marriage would be healed. Ultimately, though, he chose drugs and our marriage ended. Even so, I don't regard my marriage as a failure. Though my growth was not what I envisioned, I now know how it feels to love unconditionally. I also know what it means to be steadfast in God's presence. As my whole life came crashing down, I knew that God was with me, giving me strength, healing my heart, and helping me continue living out his purpose for my life. I pray that my ex-husband will one day be able to do the same.

Despite the disappointment and betrayal Amy faced, she never turned from the Lord. I recall seeing her kneeling in prayer, quietly calling out to God with tears streaming down her face. She didn't slander her former spouse, doubt her faith, or become bitter. Although her heart was broken, God made Amy whole again because she was fully surrendered to Him. Amy openly shares her testimony because she wants you to know that life doesn't always go according to plan and people don't always live up to expectations, but God will never betray your trust. Even if your whole world seems to be crashing down, you can find hope in your Father.

Father, thank you for your constant care and faithful love. Help me trust you more, even when life doesn't go as expected. Teach me to anchor my hope in you rather than my circumstances. Forgive me for doubting your faithfulness and questioning your goodness. Heal my heart and fill me with unconditional love. Give me the strength to forgive those who have wounded me and betrayed my trust. Fill my heart with joy and give me opportunities to share the reason for my hope, Jesus Christ. In Jesus' name, Amen.

Personal Reflection

Make a mental or written list of any unhealed wounds in your heart. Entrust each one to God, ask for complete healing, and trust him to make your heart whole. Make a decision to forgive those who have hurt you (even if your emotions don't yet line up), and pray for each of them.

_____

_____

_____

_____

_____

_____

Day 76
Boundaries

The last few days, we've talked about fostering authentic relationships and offering grace even when our kindness is not reciprocated. I'd like to take one more day to round off our discussion on the topic of boundaries. Allow me to use my dogs as an illustration.

Schnauzers are curious by nature. I know that given the opportunity, Smokey and Pepper will take off to find adventure. Thus, I keep them inside my fenced yard. The boundary prevents Smokey and Pepper from getting run over, stolen, or lost. In other words, the fence isn't punitive, but protective. Additionally, the fence safeguards our family from the emotional turmoil of a potential disaster. Because the boundary protects our dogs, we have peace even when we can't see them.

Boundaries offer greater freedom and confidence. Just as God sets boundaries in our lives to protect us from bondage to sin, sickness, and suffering, we can set boundaries in our interpersonal relationships.

The authors of the Bible offer extensive instructions about making wise decisions in regard to relational health. Although Christ calls us to have compassion and offer forgiveness, he doesn't call us to be a doormat. Our Lord desires that we prevent relational disasters and broken hearts before they happen. Solomon teaches, "Guard your heart above all else, for it determines the course of your life," (Proverbs 4:23). If the condition of our hearts can impact the course of our entire lives, we would be wise to set intentional and thoughtful boundaries around it.

So, how do we set boundaries that are healthy and God-honoring? First, prayerfully define boundaries that are protective but not punitive. Look for established patterns of behavior in your life and the lives of people around you. If certain situations tend to offend or hurt, create a boundary that protects you from that situation. Second, communicate your boundaries clearly. Express what you need, don't cast blame, and don't engage in debate. For example, "I need time to organize my thoughts," rather than, "your choices make me furious." Third, communicate the benefit of the boundary. Define how your boundary will lead to greater relational health and emotional peace for all parties. Even if your peer doesn't understand or agree, try to end the conversation by affirming that you care for them.

The final step in boundary setting is assessment. Start small and see how things go. Evaluate your success and make changes as needed. Don't be afraid to apologize if your boundary goes sideways. Start over and try something new. If you can't seem to figure it out on your own, seek professional help![7]

Lord, thank you for teaching me how to walk in relational health in increasing measure. Show me how to cultivate healthy boundaries in my life. Help me to guard my heart so that I can follow you and bear much fruit. Prepare the way before me so that my friends and family are receptive to the safeguards that need to be set in our relationships. Forgive me for allowing dysfunction to fester and guide me as I seek to take decisive action. As I seek to create healthy boundaries, help me proceed with love, grace, and kindness. In Jesus' name, Amen.

---

[7] We have only touched upon the basics of healthy boundaries. For further study, see *Boundaries* by Henry Cloud and John Townsend (Zondervan, 2017).

Personal Reflection

Begin to walk through the steps outlined above: determine the boundaries that you need, communicate them, express the benefit of honoring them, and assess. The process of setting healthy boundaries can't be completed in one day. In fact, healthy boundary maintenance is a life-long endeavor. But there is no better time to start than today!

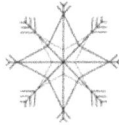

Day 77
Tex the Terror — Part 1

A couple of days ago, we touched on the topic of forgiveness. We'll spend several more days examining the topic in depth, as it is one of the most vital aspects of our spiritual walk. Yet, while forgiveness is crucial, it can also be excruciatingly difficult to practice.

Jesus' teaching on forgiveness in Matthew 6 is especially hard to digest. Jesus states, "If you forgive those who sin against you, your heavenly Father will forgive you. But if you refuse to forgive others, your Father will not forgive your sins," (Matthew 6:14–15). We don't have time for an in-depth discussion, but let me affirm that our Father will *always* forgive us when we ask with authenticity. Based on the context of Scripture and the character of God, I believe that Jesus is teaching that if our heart is too hardened to forgive others, it's also too hardened for an authentic conversation with God. Forgiveness is simply a fundamental aspect of our faith.

To illustrate the importance of forgiveness, I would like to tell you about Tex. Tex is my Mom's dog, a beautiful King Charles cavalier spaniel. Because our whole family is animal-obsessed, we were overjoyed when she decided to adopt a new puppy. We were even more delighted when we first held the adorable ball of orange and white fur with big eyes and floppy ears.

Soon after, we happily volunteered to keep Tex during Mom's vacation. The trip was still months away, so we hoped he would be house trained by then. Either way, however, we were prepared to keep a close eye on Tex and prevent any puppy-related damage—or so we thought.

As soon as the week with Tex began, we knew we'd made a grave mistake. On the first night, Tex slept in the bed with Asher, as was customary with our own dogs. Since dogs don't pee where they sleep, we felt safe. Unfortunately, our certainty was misguided, and Tex released the floodgates in Asher's bed. As if that weren't bad enough, later in the day while Asher was holding him, Tex peed right in Asher's lap. At that point, Asher was done babysitting Tex.

Despite our diligent and frequent efforts to convince Tex to urinate outside, the pee spree continued. Beds, carpets, floors—nothing was safe. In case you are wondering, Tex did not have a bladder infection. He just didn't want to "go" outside.

In addition to the pee problem, Tex rampaged through our house with the frenzy of a Tasmanian devil. He chewed up various shoes, pillows, blankets, and anything else into which he could sink his teeth. Worst of all, he gnawed the legs of our dining room table into shapeless stubs.

Although we cared for him attentively, Tex caused substantial damage during his stay in our home. My mom graciously recompensed us for the damage, but I've struggled to forgive Tex ever since. I know it seems silly that I would struggle to forgive a dog. At the time of the offense, he was only a puppy. He didn't know any better, and he didn't have malicious intent. He isn't very smart, even for a dog, and that's not his fault.

Sometimes the individual we are struggling to forgive is just as oblivious. Our offender didn't intend to hurt us, they didn't know any better, and they didn't have malicious intent. Holding a grudge only hardens our own heart and keeps us from experiencing the fullness of our faith.

On the other hand, you may be struggling to forgive someone who harmed you in ways far worse than peeing in your bed and chewing up your table. Someone may have harmed you intentionally and maliciously. Perhaps they are continuing to wound you even now. Your anger may be well justified. Yet, in asking you to forgive, God is NOT condoning the hurtful things done to you. God calls you to forgive because he knows that harboring unforgiveness harms you even further.

We'll continue talking about forgiveness tomorrow. Let's pause for today, seek God, and have an authentic conversation with our Father.

Lord, thank you for the unconditional forgiveness you've granted me. Give me the strength to forgive and extend grace to others. Reveal any individuals against whom I'm harboring unforgiveness. Show me what I can learn from those who've wronged me so that I can grow in faith and maturity. Make my heart healthy instead of hardened and help me see all people through your eyes. I pray that my example of forgiveness and grace would inspire others to become free from their own unforgiveness. In Jesus' name, Amen.

Personal Reflection

Prayerfully make a list of people against whom you are harboring unforgiveness for any offense or hurt. Ask God to help you forgive each person and begin the healing process. Even if your emotions don't yet line up, make a mental decision to forgive that is based on your love for the Father and his love for you.

Day 77

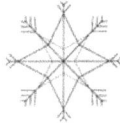

Day 78
Tex the Terror — Part 2

Today, and for the next few days, we'll continue discussing forgiveness. As a vital aspect of our faith, spiritual growth and health are dependent upon forgiveness. Conversely, unforgiveness yields spiritual stagnation and bitterness.

At times, we withhold forgiveness while waiting for our offender to repent or apologize. Unfortunately, we may never receive the hoped for penitence. Further, as we hold onto offense, we give our offender ongoing control over our mental, emotional, and spiritual well-being.

By way of illustration, I told you about my struggle to forgive Tex, who rampaged through our house leaving destruction and urine in his wake. Wouldn't it be ridiculous for me to expect an apology from Tex? As a dog, Tex lacks the verbal and cognitive skills to provide an apology. Yet, some of the people who offend us likewise lack the self-awareness and maturity to repent.

Instead of waiting for an apology that we may never receive, you and I can take responsibility for our own healing. I can repair my dining room table or continue to get angry every time I notice the damage. I can clean my carpets and wash bedding or I can bitterly endure a nasty house. Expecting Tex to clean up his mess would be irrational. Yet, expecting people who hurt us to help us heal is just as futile. Paul commands us to take responsibility for the condition of our hearts.

> *Get rid of all bitterness, rage, anger, harsh words, and*
> *slander, as well as all types of evil behavior. Instead,*

> *be kind to each other, tenderhearted, forgiving one an-*
> *other, just as God through Christ has forgiven you.*
> *Imitate God, therefore, in everything you do, because*
> *you are his dear children. Live a life filled with love,*
> *following the example of Christ.*
> ***Ephesians 5:31—6:2***

Christ forgave his enemies even as they crucified him (Luke 23:34). As Christians, imitators of Christ, our goal in life should be to emulate him.

Extending forgiveness doesn't mean that the hurt perpetrated against us was acceptable. By forgiving, we simply release ourselves from continuing bondage to bitterness. We give our hearts permission to heal and our lives freedom to flourish.

Lord, thank you for modeling forgiveness during your life, death, and resurrection. Help me to forgive those who have hurt me so that I can imitate your loving example. Rid my heart of bitterness, rage, and anger. Rid my tongue of slander, and rid my life of evil. Fill my heart with love and forgiveness toward others and teach me to extend kindness in every situation. In Jesus' name, Amen.

Personal Reflection

Yesterday, you created a list of people against whom you are harboring unforgiveness. Reaffirm your choice to extend forgiveness, even if your emotions don't yet line up. Ask God to reveal specific ways you can begin to take responsibility for your own healing. Write down a few ideas on the next page.

Day 79
Forgive and Forget?

The last few days, we've been discussing forgiveness. I fully realize that saying we *should* forgive is much easier than actually doing it. Often, we want to forgive, but we simply can't seem to move past the hurt. To help you through the healing process, I would like to discuss what forgiveness *is* and what it *is not*.

First, forgiveness is a mental decision, not an emotional response. Wanting to forgive, yet still feeling angry and hurt is totally normal. You and I simply don't have the ability to turn off emotions like a light switch. Although God has the power to heal our hearts miraculously, he most often guides us through a process of healing. As we work through our emotions, God helps us grow stronger and become healthier.

Yet, even as we grow more mentally and spiritually mature, past hurts may remain tender. An emotionally tender place in our hearts, however, doesn't equate to unforgiveness. For instance, every time I notice the rips and teeth marks in my lovely bedroom quilt, I feel a visceral flare of anger toward Tex. Instead of allowing the anger to simmer and fester, I simply remind myself that I've forgiven Tex. Similarly, you may need to reaffirm your decision to forgive on a regular basis. Your emotions may take a while to catch up, and that's ok.

Second, forgiveness is not the same as forgetting. I'm sure you've heard the phrase, "forgive and forget," but this modern-day maxim is patently umbilical and unrealistic. While our Father has the divine ability to choose to forget our sins, he typically doesn't grant us the same faculty. In fact, past traumas often constitute some of our most vivid memories. Instead of vainly trying to forget offenses, we can choose not to ruminate over the hurt and even draw upon our experience to help others.

Third, forgiveness doesn't equate to a restored relationship. Forgiveness does not require ongoing contact or continued communication. As we forgive, we should learn from our wounds and create protective boundaries for the future. In some cases, we may need to cease contact completely to protect ourselves from further harm. In other cases, we may be able to maintain a relationship, but establish appropriate safeguards. In other words, I'll play with Tex at Mom's, but he will never again stay overnight at my house! According to Proverbs 22:3, "A prudent person foresees danger and takes precautions. The simpleton goes blindly on and suffers the consequences."

Lord, thank you for healing my heart and moving me past the bondage of unforgiveness. Give me strength to maintain a mindset of forgiveness until my emotions align with my spiritual and mental decision. Show me what I can learn from my past hurts so that I can better protect myself in the future. Give me the wisdom to set healthy boundaries that honor you and foster peace in my life. Give me opportunities to help others who are struggling with past pain and unforgiveness. In Jesus' name, Amen.

Personal Reflection

Yesterday, you asked God to reveal specific ways you can begin to take responsibility for your own healing. Prayerfully review your list and begin implementing one strategy today.

Day 79

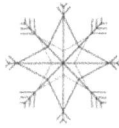

Day 80
Prayer, Perspective, and Practice

Over the last few days, we've been discussing the importance of forgiveness. To help you navigate the healing process, we'll spend two final days on practical strategies for letting go of offense. For ease of memory, I'll give you three "P"s today and three "R"s tomorrow. Because I want you to hear the voice of God more than my own, both days will be saturated with Scripture.

First, *prayer* must be our priority. Obviously, we will pray for our own healing. Perhaps even more effective, however, we'll pray for the people who have hurt or offended us. Jesus instructs, "But I say, love your enemies! Pray for those who persecute you! In that way, you will be acting as true children of your Father in heaven," (Matthew 5:44–45).

As we pray for our enemies, our hearts begin to soften. Jesus helps us see the people who hurt us as flawed humans rather than dimensionless beings of pure evil. He enables us to offer compassion rather than contempt.

Second, adjusting our *perspective* facilitates healing. Despite the harmful actions perpetrated against us or the hurtful words spoken about us, God offers fresh blessings each day. Instead of dwelling upon past hurts, we can be present for the blessings today holds. We can focus our attention on the beauty in the world, the kindness of others, and even the good in those who've hurt us.

Another perspective adjustment entails our identity. We must remember that our identity is not characterized by victimhood, and that the identity of our offender is not characterized by their hurtful actions. According to Paul, "For we are not fighting against flesh-and-blood enemies, but against evil rulers and authorities of the unseen world, against mighty powers in this dark world, and against evil spirits in the heavenly places," (Ephesians 6:12). Paul teaches that other people are not our enemies. Even if someone's actions are influenced by evil entities, we can have compassion on their condition and pray for their freedom.

Third, we must *practice* the discipline of forgiveness. Matthew recounts Peter's question, ""Lord, how often should I forgive someone who sins against me? Seven times?" "No, not seven times," Jesus replied, "but seventy times seven!"" (Matthew 18:21–22). In other words, Jesus calls us to forgive as often as we are offended. The number of times we are hurt should dictate the number of times we forgive. Even if the same person inflicts harm time and time again, Jesus still calls us to forgive. (Although we should also set healthy boundaries to prevent further hurt.)

As we forgive, we should also practice compassion, empathy, and kindness. In fact, compassion, empathy, and kindness are closely related to forgiveness. All are facets of God's love and each facilitates the other. When our lives are characterized by God's love, unforgiveness simply can't take root.

Lord, thank you for extending kindness, grace, and forgiveness to me. Help me extend the same to others. Teach me to release offense and see my offender through your eyes. Fix my gaze on the good in others and the beauty in the world. Fill my heart with gratitude instead of grudges. Give me the capacity to forgive as many times as needed so that bitterness can't take root in my heart. Grow my spiritual discernment so that I can fight against the schemes of the enemy rather than fellow humans created in your image. In Jesus' name, Amen.

Personal Reflection

Review and revise (if needed), the list of people against whom you are harboring unforgiveness. Reaffirm your choice to extend forgiveness, and pray for each person on your list.

_____

_____

_____

_____

_____

_____

_____

_____

_____

_____

_____

_____

_____

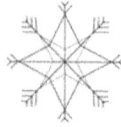

Day 81

Reflection, Responsibility, and Reconciliation

Today is our final discussion of forgiveness. Yesterday, I gave you three practical strategies for letting go of offense: prayer, perspective, and practice. Today, I'll give you three more: reflection, responsibility, and reconciliation. You don't have to work through the "P"s and "R"s in any particular order, but prayer should accompany all of them.

The first "R" is *reflection*. Our first instinct is to react when we face trauma, hurt, or offense. If we touch a hot stove, we jerk our hand away. If we trip, we reach out to steady ourselves. If we stub a toe, we scream—or at least, I will.

Our reflexive reactions often protect us or signal that we need help, but sometimes they make our situation worse. For example, when another person inflicts harm upon us, our instinct is to retaliate. Instead, Jesus teaches, "Do not resist an evil person! If someone slaps you on the right cheek, offer the other cheek also," (Matthew 5:39). Paul further instructs, "Never pay back evil with more evil. Do things in such a way that everyone can see you are honorable," (Romans 12:17).

By practicing the discipline of reflection, we can create a habit of responding instead of reacting. When we reflect, we prayerfully evaluate the situation. We consider the words and actions of our offender. We examine our own thoughts and feelings. We evaluate the signals our emotions are sending. Then, rather than acting on impulse, we embark upon a wise course of action that honors God and fosters health rather than reaping the short-term satisfaction of revenge.

Our second "R" is *responsibility*. Casting blame is easier than taking responsibility for our own mistakes. John records this well-known interaction between Jesus and the pharisees.

> *"Teacher," they said to Jesus, "this woman was caught in the act of adultery. The law of Moses says to stone her. What do you say?" They were trying to trap him into saying something they could use against him, but Jesus stooped down and wrote in the dust with his finger. They kept demanding an answer, so he stood up again and said, "All right, but let the one who has never sinned throw the first stone!"*
>
> **John 8:4–7**

Blame sows bitterness and unforgiveness while taking responsibility empowers us to learn and grow. Acknowledging our own complicity is essential for healing.

Even if we prayerfully determine that we are truly innocent in the situation at hand, we should still remember that we all have shortcomings and have likely hurt others at times. Paul reminds us that "Everyone has sinned; we all fall short of God's glorious standard," (Romans 3:23). Lest you lean too much into self-condemnation, though, remember that you also have a responsibility to extend compassion and forgiveness to yourself. God already has!

Our third and final "R" is *reconciliation*. According to Hebrews 12, we should "Work at living in peace with everyone, and work at living a holy life, for those who are not holy will not see the Lord. Look after each other so that none of you fails to receive the grace of God. Watch out that no poisonous root of bitterness grows up to trouble you, corrupting many," (Hebrews 12:14–15). Unforgiveness and unresolved anger pull us away from God's heart, catalyze bitterness in our own hearts, and corrupt the hearts of others.

Reconciliation will look different in each situation. In some cases, compassion, kindness, and mutual understanding can lead to fully restored relationships. In other cases, reconciliation can occur, but with new boundaries in place. Sadly, some situations require reconciliation without an ongoing relationship.

If you prayerfully determine that further contact will be unproductive or dangerous, reconciliation will be more spiritual, mental, and emotional than relational. Your reconciliation might begin by writing a letter to the person who abused you, yet never delivering it. Your restoration may be accomplished by helping others through similar trials. Your healing may happen through setting healthy boundaries, making new plans, and moving into a new season of life.

Although reconciliation and restoration will look different in every case, the love of God and the support of other people will always be part of the process. If forgiveness continues to be a struggle, consult a spiritual mentor and a professional counselor to guide you toward healing and health.

Lord, thank you for the emotions and experiences that enhance my life. Teach me to evaluate my emotions and experiences so that I can better understand myself and the people in my life. Help me respond with wisdom rather than reacting without thought. Show me whether I bear any responsibility for the hurts I've experienced. As I acknowledge that I have made my own mistakes, give me greater compassion toward those who've hurt me. Guide me as I seek to forgive myself and reconcile with others. In Jesus' name, Amen.

Personal Reflection

Consider the three "R"s: reflection, responsibility, and reconciliation. Prayerfully determine which is the most difficult for you then practice it throughout your day. Remember to cover each thought, word, and action in prayer.

_____

_____

_____

_____

_____

_____

_____

_____

_____

_____

_____

_____

_____

_____

Day 82
Lenten Roses

I have a large patch of lenten roses in one of my flower beds. The plants have no relation to actual roses; they get the name because the flowers look somewhat like roses, and they bloom most heavily during the season of Lent. They do, however, bloom all year long if kept well pruned. Unpruned, the roots will continue pumping nutrients into stalks, leaves, and flowers that are dying. New growth is unlikely because the old growth is absorbing all of the resources.

Often, God wants to do something new through us, but we are holding so tightly to the past that we don't have the capacity to move into a new season or a new direction. Perhaps God wants to prune a harmful habit, self-destructive behavior, or an unhealthy tendency. Perhaps he wants to prune a relationship. Perhaps he even wants to prune something beautiful that brought honor to Him and blessed other people. Just because God is moving you into a new season of life or ministry doesn't invalidate the previous one.

If we aren't willing to let go of the past when He calls us to move forward, we will continue utilizing resources (time, money, energy), while our growth begins to slow and eventually stop. In Ecclesiastes, we learn that "There is a time for everything, and a season for every activity under the heavens: a time to be born and a time to die, a time to plant and a time to uproot," (Ecclesiastes 3:1–2). Unless we allow God to prune our lives, we won't have enough resources left over for new growth.

Jesus was human like us, and he faced many opportunities to reject God's pruning hand. What if He hadn't been willing to transition from the safety of his home into a season of itinerant public ministry? Or what if he had said, "God my ministry is really starting to take off. I don't want to go to the Cross,"? Instead, Jesus was ready each time God called Him into a new season. Jesus faced the ultimate pruning—sacrificing his own life so that we, his followers, could experience newness of life.

Lord, I ask you to examine my heart. Reveal any areas of my life that are not fully submitted to you. Show me any patterns of thought, speech, or behavior that dishonor you. Give me the strength to obey when you ask me to prune anything that might be harming my relationship with you or others. Help me to be sensitive to your guidance and follow your direction when you lead me into new seasons of life and ministry. Thank you for your constant guiding hand in my life. Grant me the maturity to accept your pruning, even when it is uncomfortable. Amen.

Personal Reflection

Take some time today to reflect on what might need pruning in your life. Ask yourself the following questions as you listen for God's voice.

- Does God desire to prune an area of your life that is harming your relationship with him or others?
- Is God calling you to prune any patterns of thought, speech, or behavior?
- Is God calling you to redirect any resources to make room for new opportunities to flourish?

Day 82

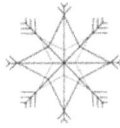

Day 83
Mardi Gras Beads

By now you're likely in Lent, whether or not you observe the season, which is traditionally 40 days of self-sacrifice and solemn contemplation on the death and resurrection of Christ. Mardi Gras, commemorated most notably in New Orleans, marks the last opportunity to party before Lent begins. During the N'awlins festivities, bead necklaces get thrown everywhere. Occupants of parade floats, in particular, toss handfuls of the colorful strands to people in the crowd. So many beads get flung through the air that the necklaces end up draped over the branches of the beautiful live oaks that line the streets. During the party, the beads add to the air of celebration. After the festivities end, however, the beads begin to fade. Instead of adorning the trees with color, the tangled-up necklaces make the stately trees look trashy and dirty.

Whenever I see the faded old beads hanging forlornly in the trees, I think of the way sin works in our lives. Initially, vice might seem exciting and desirable. We're tempted to indulge because sin appears fulfilling and fun. We anticipate more happiness, contentment, success, productivity. . . . You get the point. Ultimately, though, our enjoyment fades, and we're left with the ugly aftermath.

In truth, sin *never* brings more joy, only suffering. When the enemy tempts us, his goal is to steal, kill, and destroy (John 10:10). When we follow him into temptation, the baubles that seemed bright and shiny turn into bondage and shame. Like the beads caught in the trees, we are tangled up and entrapped by our sin.

God, however, wants to give us freedom and life unencumbered by temporary treasures. The author of Hebrews exhorts, "Let us lay aside every impediment and the sin that easily entangles us; let us run with patient endurance the race which is set before us," (Hebrews 12:1, my translation).

When we lay aside sin, resist temptation, and abide in God's presence, we have access to joy that never fades. Instead of fleeting pleasure, we receive unending life. In fact, anything outside of the love of our Father, his plan for our lives, and the fruit of our relationship with him will ultimately pass away. Isaiah proclaims, "The grass withers and the flowers fade, but the word of our God stands forever," (Isaiah 40:8).

Next time you're tempted to sin, think of those dirty old beads hanging in the trees. Remind yourself that sin brings only fading pleasure and bondage, but God's presence brings joy and freedom everlasting (Psalm 16:11).

Heavenly Father, thank you for giving me life and freedom. Help me avoid the snares of the enemy and resist temptation. Give me the fortitude to lay aside every sin that encumbers my life of faith. I know that your plans are for good while the plans of the enemy are for destruction. Grant me the wisdom to see through the deception of the enemy and walk in your truth. Help me abide in your Word so that I'm able to discern truth from lies. Thank you for giving me eternal salvation and joy that never fades. In Jesus' name, Amen.

Personal Reflection

Meditate on your personal holiness. Are you allowing the temptation and deception of the enemy to impede your walk with Christ?

Prayerfully ask God to show you any areas in which you might be tempted or entangled. Make a mental or written list, then spend time praying over each item. Repent of your sin, ask God to show you the outcome of each temptation, and ask him to reveal how you can replace each encumbrance with something of true and lasting value.

_____

_____

_____

_____

_____

_____

_____

_____

_____

_____

_____

_____

_____

_____

_____

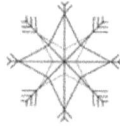

Day 84

The Velvet Cactus

The Velvet Cactus is a restaurant in New Orleans, and it's my favorite restaurant in the world. The cuisine, a fusion of Cajun and Mexican, is so good it makes me want to cry. Some of the culinary combinations are strange, but trust me, they never disappoint. I mean, where else can you order cheese grits, brussels sprouts, guacamole, and tacos on one plate?

Like the Velvet Cactus, God can use unusual pairings to create amazing things. He has taught me this principle through my own marriage. I'm loud, outgoing, and impulsive. My husband, Wesley, is quiet, calm, and thoughtful. Strictly speaking, we don't sound like a good match. Yet, we balance each other perfectly. He helps me slow down, be patient, and react calmly in stressful situations. I help him try new things, meet new people, and step out of his comfort zone.

In Scripture, we find numerous examples of unusual combinations. God empowered Ruth, a former pagan, to bear the great-grand-father of David and forever be ensconced in the lineage of Christ (Ruth 4:13–22; Matthew 1:5–16). David himself, a humble shepherd and the youngest of seven brothers, became the most prominent king in Israel's history (1 Samuel 16:6–13). God called Moses, who couldn't speak well, to be the spokesman for the entire nation of Israel (Exodus 4:10–12). God used a donkey to speak to Balaam and a fish to get Jonah's attention. Most striking of all, God sent his own son not to conquer, but to suffer and die.

Although you and I can't be certain of how God will work in our lives, we should expect the unexpected. Our Father might call us to take a surprising step of faith, interact with unlikely people, or use skills we don't yet possess. Even if his plan doesn't make sense to us, God knows what he is doing. He says in Isaiah 55:8–9, "My thoughts are nothing like your thoughts . . . And my ways are far beyond anything you could imagine. For just as the heavens are higher than the earth, so my ways are higher than your ways and my thoughts higher than your thoughts."

Our Heavenly Father cares for us intimately and has the knowledge and power to guide us successfully through life. We can trust him even when he works in mysterious ways. I know from experience that his unexpected pairings and plans are even better than dinner at the Velvet Cactus, and that is high praise!

Lord, thank you for creating amazing plans in unexpected places. Open my eyes to the opportunities around me. Help me be creative in seeking solutions to the problems in my life and community. Give me the ingenuity to use every resource at my disposal for the benefit of your kingdom and your people. Forgive me for discounting unconventional avenues of service and ministry. Help me trust and obey you even when your plan doesn't seem to make sense. Thank you for helping me step out of my comfort zone and grow in faith. In Jesus' Name, Amen

Personal Reflection

Think out of the box and brainstorm some creative ways you can serve your family, friends, and Father. Prayerfully choose one to try in the near future.

_____

_____

Day 84

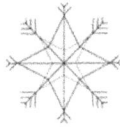

Day 85
Sweet Smelling Aroma

As we transition into spring, the scents of the season also begin to change. The aroma of fall leaves, Christmas cookies, peppermint lattes, and holiday meals will soon be replaced by the scent of blooming blossoms, swimming pools, sandy beaches, and cook-outs.

Our sense of smell is one of only five senses that we possess and one of the most powerful ways that we experience the world around us and. The ability to detect different scents empowers us to enjoy our environment and safely navigate our surroundings. Or if I smell smoke, I know that something is probably burning. If I smell something nasty in my fridge, I know that I need to find the food that has gone bad!

Certain smells can evoke powerful memories or associations. My Pops drank coffee non-stop, so when I smell coffee, I feel like my Pops is near. My Gram loved gardenias. She grew them around the house, and when the bushes were in bloom, she would bring blossoms inside so that the house smelled like them. So, when I smell gardenias, I reflect on wonderful memories of my Gram.

I think that the apostle Paul understood the power of smell. In 2 Corinthians 2:14–15, he exclaims:

But thanks be to God! For through what Christ has done, he has triumphed over us so that now wherever we go he uses us to tell others about the Lord and to spread the Gospel like a sweet perfume. As far as God is concerned there is a sweet, wholesome fragrance in our lives. It is the fragrance of Christ within us, an aroma to both the saved and the unsaved all around us.

In these verses from 2 Corinthians, Paul explains that we, as Christ followers, have an aroma! When we have a relationship with Jesus, we begin to "smell" like him. As a result, when people encounter us, they can begin to experience Jesus. When we smell like Jesus, we exude a fragrance of love, joy, peace, and kindness. Paul describes the scent as a sweet perfume that everyone around us can enjoy. More importantly, the sweet-smelling aroma of Christ attracts people toward a relationship with him.

Sometimes, especially during times of turmoil in our world, we are tempted to withdraw from others. We hide within our bubble of safety and familiarity because the world can be a scary place. Yet, times of trial are precisely when the aroma of Christ is most needed. God has called us to step outside of our bubble and share the aroma of Christ with our peers—family, friends, colleagues, even enemies.

Let's douse ourselves in the fragrance of Christ like an old man puts on cologne. Let that scent be so strong that everyone in the room can smell your love, joy, and compassion. Then, as we share the sweet aroma of God's love, we might just get the opportunity to share the reason for our hope—Jesus himself.

Jesus, thank you for covering me with your love even when I smell like sin. I ask you to cover me in the sweet-smelling aroma of the Gospel at all times. Bring people across my path who need to experience the fragrance of Christ. Open doors of opportunity for me to share the Gospel with those who are far from your love and grace. Guide my interactions and give me the right words to speak at the right moment. In Jesus' name, Amen.

Personal Reflection

What do you "smell" like? Does your life give off the aroma of Christ or do you smell like the world? Are your words and actions drawing other people nearer to God's love and Christ's salvation? Do you actively look for opportunities to share the sweet aroma of Christ?

_____

_____

_____

_____

_____

_____

_____

_____

_____

_____

_____

_____

_____

_____

Day 86
Sustainable Stewardship — Part 1

Today and tomorrow, I would like to discuss a topic that is near and dear to my heart. I'm certain you won't be surprised to learn that I am passionate about environmental stewardship. Sadly, our Christian faith has often been accused of pitting humans against the natural world, and for good reason. Many Christ followers don't believe that creation care is part of the Gospel or relevant to spiritual growth. To the contrary, our faith is inherently connected to the world in which we live. The very purpose for which we were created is to rule over creation on behalf of our Creator.

So God created human beings in his own image.
In the image of God he created them;
male and female he created them.
Then God blessed them and said, "Be fruitful and
multiply. Fill the earth and govern it. Reign over the
fish in the sea, the birds in the sky, and all the ani-
mals that scurry along the ground."
Genesis 1:27–28

As God's stewards, we are called to care for creation with compassion and utilize our resources with wisdom. We must cultivate the health and flourishing of the natural world because it is a primary element of our purpose and because our own health is tied to that of our home.

Environmental stewardship is a vital, if neglected, aspect of salvation. The well-intentioned but misguided focus on an other-worldly, disembodied heaven has distanced us from our environment and distracted us from our calling. Jesus didn't merely sacrifice himself to save us from sin, but to redeem and restore all of creation. N. T. Wright, arguably the most brilliant living Bible scholar, laments that many Christians have settled for a "truncated and distorted version" of the greatest of all biblical expectations.[8] Salvation is not solely about rescue from death, the promise of heaven, or even a relationship with God. Salvation includes the healing of all of creation and is as broad as creation itself.

A mature faith in Christ thus involves respect for the natural world and the wonders it holds. As we grow in submission to our Lord, we should also grow more sensitive to all forms of life and increasingly recognize our interdependence. Christian environmentalism is not naive utopianism, but rather a multi-faceted response to industrial progress, developing technology, and personal choice. As followers of Christ, we are called to be agents of redemption by caring for our world and bearing the Good News of Christ's love to those who live in it.

Heavenly Father, thank you for the beautiful environment you created for your children. I'm honored you have entrusted me with caring for the natural world. Forgive me for taking lightly my responsibility in regard to the environment. Give me the wisdom and self-discipline to steward your creation well. Teach me to appreciate the fullness of the Gospel and embody the fullness of Christ's redemptive work. In Jesus' name, Amen.

---

8 N. T. Wright, *Surprised by Hope: Rethinking Heaven, the Resurrection, and the Mission of the Church* (New York: HarperOne, 2008), 19.

Personal Reflection

Reflect on your own attitude toward the natural world. Is environmental stewardship a new concept for you? Do you feel empowered or frustrated by God's call to care for creation? How can you more fully promote the redemptive work of Christ in your environment and among your peers? Write down your thoughts so you can reference them tomorrow.

_____

_____

_____

_____

_____

_____

_____

_____

_____

_____

_____

_____

_____

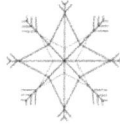

Day 87
Sustainable Stewardship — Part 2

In the 2013 film *Snowpiercer*, a catastrophic attempt to reverse global warming triggers an ice age that wipes out nearly all life on earth. The only survivors consist of a lucky few who board a perpetual-motion train that serves as a futuristic Noah's Ark. The remnant struggles to survive as confined spaces and limited resources draw the worst impulses of humanity to the surface. Even *Snowpiercer*'s train, the pinnacle of human innovation, eventually derails under the weight of human folly.

Although a secular film, the movie highlights the sin nature that leads humans to abuse creation and mistreat each other. We continue to strive for more and hoard our resources even though most of us don't worry over having enough to survive. We prioritize our own wants, often regardless of the impact on fellow creatures and the natural world. While God's creation has the capacity to sustain all life, the earth was not intended to sustain the kind of excess in which we consistently indulge.

Fortunately, when humans reflect the image of God by caring for fellow creatures and the land, the natural resources of the world will flourish and God's plan of redemption will reach its fullest expression. The author of Proverbs has much to say about environmental stewardship. He admonishes:

> *Know well the condition of your flocks,*
> *And pay attention to your herds;*

For riches are not forever,
Nor does a crown endure to all generations.
When the grass disappears, the new growth is seen,
And the herbs of the mountains are gathered in,
The lambs will be for your clothing,
And the goats will bring the price of a field,
And there will be goats' milk enough for your food,
For the food of your household,
And sustenance for your maidens.
Proverbs 27:23–27

We reflect the image of God and fulfill our calling when we move all of creation towards its fullest potential. Our stewardship should reflect God's dominion in a relationship of symbiotic care more so than an economy of use. As we discussed yesterday, Christian environmentalism is not naive utopianism or an attempt to hamper technological progress. Instead, wise stewardship consists of a multifaceted response to industrial progress, developing technology, and personal choice.

Unfortunately, I can't tell you what to do or how to do it. In our global economy, discerning which actions will have a positive impact and which will bear unseen consequences is nearly impossible. I will, however, share a few guiding principles and personal choices of my own. First, I seek to bring order and purpose to my home terrain. By making the environment around me beautiful, I hope to foster appreciation for God's handiwork. By growing my own vegetables and using a bare minimum of pesticide, I hope to foster health in my family and my living space. Second, I produce as little waste as possible and reuse as much as possible. So many of the items we routinely discard can be repurposed. While the efficacy of traditional recycling is debatable, repurposing directly reduces waste and saves money at the same time! Third, I seek to buy products that are sustainable, at least to the best of my knowledge. Sustainably sourced goods and foods typically cost more, but making sacrifices so that I can afford them is one aspect of my stewardship. Finally, I strive to be kind to all creatures—human, animal, and otherwise. Proverbs 12:10a says "A righteous man has regard for the life of his animal," and I am happy to oblige.

Even if you don't change the world, you can make a few positive changes in your own life. Moreover, if we all share the responsibility of wise stewardship, our simple efforts can yield massive change.

Heavenly Father, Thank you for creating an environment that sustains your children. Forgive me for putting my own selfish desires ahead of the good of the natural world and my fellow humans. Give me the self-discipline to make sacrifices that honor you and your creation. Help me to set an example of caring stewardship and selfless decisions. Grow my capacity for wisdom and discernment in the midst of confusing options and ambiguous outcomes. Empower me to do my best and entrust you with the results. In Jesus' name, Amen.

Personal Reflection

Once again reflect on your own attitude toward stewardship of the natural world. Review your notes from yesterday and prayerfully consider strategies for better creation care. Decide what change(s) you are going to make and begin to implement them today!

_____

_____

_____

_____

Day 87

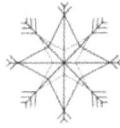

Day 88
Who Are You?

The benefits of living out the principles in God's Word become more evident to me with each passing year. The older I get, the more I embrace the practical wisdom found especially in Psalms and Proverbs. I'm truly awestruck that the ancient truths are just as impactful and relevant today as they were thousands of years ago. I was, therefore, confused when I recently read a Psalm that seemed less than accurate.

Psalm 26 is a beautiful composition in which David praises the Lord and, seemingly, his own integrity. David prays, "Declare me innocent, O Lord, for I have acted with integrity; I have trusted in the Lord without wavering. Put me on trial, Lord, and cross-examine me. Test my motives and my heart," (Psalm 26:1–2).

Although I've read the Psalm numerous times in the past, the words struck me differently this time. Having just written the previous devotionals about David's potpourri of transgressions, I struggled to accept his testimony of righteousness. In Psalm 26, David claims to possess unwavering faith and integrity, but his actions have told a different story. Even if David had written the Psalm prior to his worst infractions, the self-praise still felt arrogant to me. Yet, that doesn't seem like the David I usually encounter in scripture. So, I shifted into scholar mode for a closer look at the passage.

As soon as I opened my Hebrew Bible, David's words came into focus. David's claim to have "acted with integrity" loses something in translation. In Hebrew, the phrase echoes the language of God's

commands to Israel—not just the first ten, but the entire intercon-
nected body of legal, social, and spiritual statutes. The word *tam*, translated above as "integrity," more accurately describes the state required
for sacrificial offerings. Although *tam* can denote moral goodness in
the right context, David clearly uses the word in a temple setting. In
other words, David presents himself as an offering that is whole, without blemish, and fully surrendered to the Lord. In verse 6, David declares, "I wash my hands to declare my innocence. I come to your
altar, O Lord," (Psalm 26:6). Like a priest, he washes his hands before
approaching the altar, but the sacrifice he offers is himself.

Sacrifices wholly devoted to God, if they were acceptable, would
atone for the sins of the offeror. The entire process was just as trans-
actional as it was relational. God's forgiveness took the form of a legal
declaration that was granted if the sacrifice was worthy. Well aware of
such proceedings, David requests a legal declaration of righteousness
based on his complete devotion to God. He isn't truly innocent, but
he prays that God will declare him so.

In sum, David isn't making a statement about his righteousness,
but about his identity. The future king declares that he has made an
intentional choice to align himself with Yahweh. Rather than attend-
ing the gatherings of sinful men, David has chosen to spend time
with God's people in the temple. Instead of speaking words of pride
and falsehood, David has chosen to sing songs of praise. Instead of
dirtying his hands with evil schemes, David has chosen to wash his
hands clean.

Psalm 26 beautifully illustrates a truth we often forget. God doesn't
require a perfect life, only a fully surrendered heart. Trying harder to
follow the rules will never make us right with God or earn his favor.
When our hearts are fully surrendered, however, we lean into his process of transformation. We begin to live according to the standards of
our Father because of his love for us and our love for him.

God has freely given us his love, a principle which David understood well. Even as David petitioned God for mercy, he sang words of thanksgiving and praise in confident knowledge of his Father's faithfulness.

Lord, thank you for accepting my imperfections and making me whole. Words can't express the depth of my gratitude for your sacrifice on my behalf. Remove any inclinations in my heart that are preventing me from being fully surrendered to you. Take away any desires that don't honor you and replace them with a desire for more of your presence. Give me the courage to confidently and publicly declare my identity in you. Teach me how to walk in obedience without losing sight of your love and grace. In Jesus' name, Amen.

Personal Reflection

Reflect on your own identity and ask yourself the question, "Who are you?" Meditate and consider whether your identity is more firmly rooted in God or some other aspect of your life—your profession, your role as a spouse or parent, a hobby, a relationship, your sexual orientation, a physical trait, a psychological condition or a medical diagnosis. Our culture wants to define us by these traits, many of which can change, some of which are honorable, and some of which disregard the Lordship of Jesus in our life. Remember that the standards and preferences of our culture change, but our Father never will. Before you conclude your devotional time for today, pray for the Father to transform your mind and heart until your life is fully surrendered to him and your identity is firmly rooted in him.

Day 88

_____
_____
_____
_____
_____
_____
_____
_____
_____
_____
_____
_____
_____
_____
_____
_____
_____
_____

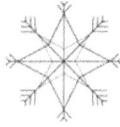

Day 89
Who Is God?

Yesterday we took a deep dive into Psalm 26 and David's wholehearted devotion to God. At first glance, David appears to praise his own integrity. A closer examination, however, reveals that David is declaring himself a fully devoted servant whose identity is rooted in God.

As David makes a statement about his own identity, he also testifies to the character of God. David can declare that he is innocent not because he is sinless, but because the Father is faithful. God is not capricious, deceptive, or unreliable like the evil men that David avoids. Rather, the Lord is trustworthy, loving, and constant. David declares, "For I am always aware of your unfailing love," (Psalm 26:3a).

In keeping with the context we discussed yesterday, David describes God's love in terms of contractual obligation: *hesed.* I realize that viewing our relationship with God in terms of a legal contract is off-putting to modern sensibilities. However, the peoples surrounding Israel believed in gods who were unpredictable, manipulative, and aloof. Worshippers could never be certain how to earn the favor of their deities or appease their fickle whims. Devotees hoped for the protection and provision of their god, but they certainly couldn't depend on it.

Thus, in the context of the ancient world, God's covenant with Israel was an unparalleled gift. No longer did the people have to wonder how to worship the Lord or worry whether he would protect them. God promised his people a different kind of relationship—one based on *hesed*. Though *hesed* does bear the nuance of obligation, the term also carries the idea that God loves to fulfill his promises because he loves his children.

As with David and the people of ancient Israel, our relationship with our Father is fundamentally rooted in his *hesed*. God's love will never cease and his character will never change. Unlike the morals and standards of our culture, which constantly shift, God provides timeless principles around which we can order our lives. Our Father, in his kindness, provides solid ground in which we can safely anchor our identity. I pray that, like David, we'll confidently stand upon God's faithfulness and declare our identity as a child of God.

Father, I praise you for your faithful love and protection. Thank you for providing a firm foundation in which I can anchor my identity. I repent of doubting you and rooting my identity in other places. I pray that you would continue to deepen my understanding of your character and your love. Teach me to walk in obedience out of my love for you instead of legalism or fear. Give me the courage to publicly declare my faith, and provide opportunities for me to share your love with others. In Jesus' name, Amen

Personal Reflection

Read Psalm 26 and then write your own version. It doesn't have to be poetic or elegant. Simply describe yourself in the light of God's love and praise God for the ways he has made you whole.

Scan the QR code for passages of Scripture

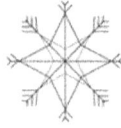

Day 90
Winds of Change

Times change, seasons change, and feelings change, but God never changes. Countless passages of Scripture describe the unchanging character of God and his son, Jesus Christ. Humans, however, change constantly. Our physical bodies grow from infancy to adulthood, then continue to change as we age. Our minds change as we acquire knowledge, learn about the world, and interact with our surroundings. Our emotions change as we develop relationships, which also evolve over time. Our skills, jobs, routines, habits, and hobbies all change. Our souls even change as we develop a relationship with the Lord and grow in Christ.

Despite the constancy of change, we all resist it to some degree. Although we eagerly anticipate some changes like marriage and retirement, we often fear the uncertainty of different seasons and experiences. We even sometimes dread changes that are natural and desirable. For instance, the thought of my boys growing up and moving away turns me into a sobbing mess.

Ironically, I hadn't even planned on having children. I shared in an Autumn devotional that I was devastated upon finding out I was pregnant and terrified about the changes children would bring to my life. I was furious with God as I mourned the loss of my future—at least the future I had planned. I now know that Asher and Abel, the most frightening changes of my entire life, are also the greatest blessing I've ever experienced. God wasn't taking anything away from me, he was giving me a wonderful gift.

At the root, fear of change boils down to a lack of trust in God. With our limited human knowledge and understanding, we simply can't predict what will happen next and we can't control the outcome. If I am trusting in my own unreliable knowledge and skills, my fears are justified. I can barely get through the day without tripping over my own feet. If, however, I trust in God, I can walk with peace and hope. Through faith, my life is securely rooted in the foundation of my Father, one who is firmer than the very foundations of the earth. David proclaims,

> *Long ago you laid the foundation of the earth*
> *and made the heavens with your hands.*
> *They will perish, but you remain forever;*
> *they will wear out like old clothing.*
> *You will change them like a garment*
> *and discard them.*
> *But you are always the same;*
> *you will live forever.*
> *The children of your people*
> *will live in security.*
> *Their children's children*
> *will thrive in your presence.*
> ***Psalm 102:25–28***

We can embrace change and look forward to new seasons because our Father never changes. Even when we face unexpected shifts and unwanted trials, God is still faithful. He is always kind, he never abandons us, and his love endures forever. Whether we are simply transitioning into the spring or into a whole new season of life, let's walk with confidence and thrive in the presence of our Father!

Father, thank you for your steadfast love and faithful care. Forgive me for fearing the future and doubting your wisdom. Grow my faith so that I learn to face every change and challenge with hope. Help me to trust you even when my life takes an unexpected turn. I acknowledge that you know every detail about my future even when I don't. Show me how to remain in the center of your will, make the most of every season, and embrace your plan to the fullest. In Jesus' name, Amen

Personal Reflection

What are you looking forward to in your next season of life? What, if any, fears do you have about your future? Pray and release each situation to the Lord. Commit your worries to his care and confess your trust in his faithfulness. Consider memorizing Psalm 102:25–28 so that when fear of the future tries to trip you, you can remain rooted and flourishing in your faith.

_____

_____

_____

_____

_____

_____

_____

_____